3 Steps

To Become a Millionaire

An Easy-to-Follow Age-based Method

Dr. Yong Q

ISBN: 979-8-9896541-0-9

DISCLAIMER

This publication contains the opinions and ideas of its authors. It is not a recommendation to buy or sell the investment or any of the funds or companies herein discussed. This publication is sold with the understanding that the authors and the publishers are not engaged in providing legal, investment, accounting, or other professional services. Laws vary from State to State and from Countries to Countries, local and/or federal laws may apply to a particular investment, and if the readers need expert financial or other services or legal advice, a competent professional should be consulted.

Neither the authors nor the publishers can guarantee the accuracy of the information contained herein. The authors and the publishers cannot control and are not responsible for the content, accuracy, or completeness of the information cited herein or of third-party websites. The examples and mathematical simulations are for illustrations only. Past returns may not be an indication of future performance.

The authors are not licensed investment professionals. The methodology and approaches outlined in this book are acquired through self-learning and self-education. The methodology and approaches outlined in this book may not be suitable for every individual and are not guaranteed or warranted to produce any specific results. The methods outlined in this book are not guaranteed or warranted to make you a millionaire or a multi-millionaire.

There are many risks associated with investment, including but not limited to: (1) loss of money or loss of principal; (2) an investment return that is below desired annual rate of return or below average market return; (3) an investment return that is below the annual rate of inflation; (4) tax related complications; (5) additional time and stress coming along with managing investments, etc.

The authors and the publishers specifically disclaim any responsibility for any liabilities, loss, or risk, professional or otherwise, which is incurred as a result, directly or indirectly, of the use and application of any of the contents of this book.

Contents

ACKNOWLEDGMENTS

I am grateful for the support my parents gave to me for my education and for the support of my wife and my children that allows me to spend countless hours on self-learning investing. A special thanks to my daughters Cindy and Lucy who helped to design the wonderful book covers.

INTRODUCTION

According to a recent survey, the total number of millionaires in the USA is about 22 million, or just about 6.5% of the 340 million USA population. And only about 1% of the world population are millionaires.

I have a mixed feeling on this data: On one hand, I am sad that just about 6.5 people out of 100 people in the USA, or about 1 person out of 100 people in the world, are millionaires, because virtually everyone can become a millionaire based on my own experience and an easy-to-follow 3-step method from my research and discovery as detailed in this book.

However, on the other hand, I am extremely excited about the positive impact of this book could potentially have: that more than 93% of the people in the USA, and about 99% of the people in the world, could potentially become a millionaire or a multi-millionaire by taking advantage of this simple and easy-to-follow 3-step method as detailed in this book.

Before we get into the details of this easy-to-follow 3-step method, let us look at a few possible pathways to become a millionaire:

(1) You could be a millionaire or a multi-millionaire if you are a lucky lottery winner. However, the chance of winning a lottery is extremely low: according to the lottery website, if you were to play Powerball in the USA ($2 per ticket), the odds of winning $1 million are 1 in about 11 million, odds of winning a jackpot are 1 in about 292 million. If you were to play Mega Million in the USA ($2 per ticket), the odds of winning $1 million are 1 in ~12 million, the odds of winning a jackpot are 1 in ~302 million. Clearly, we cannot count on playing lottery to become a millionaire.

(2) If you are born into a wealthy family, you may become a millionaire or a multi-millionaire by inheritance from your wealthy family.

(3) You could become a millionaire or multi-millionaire by becoming a celebrity (such as Hollywood movie or TV celebrities, sports stars, pop singers, etc.)

(4) You could become a millionaire or a multi-millionaire by being successful in your own businesses or being successful in climbing to the top of the corporate ladder, such as becoming a CEO, etc.

You may have already realized, only a limited number of people may be lucky enough to become a millionaire or a multi-millionaire from these 4 possible pathways. If you are like me, an ordinary working-class person, how can we become a millionaire? Do you just give up and say that "I am never going to become a millionaire, let alone a multi-millionaire?" No, not so fast! Virtually everyone can become a millionaire or a multi-millionaire, by simply following an easy 3-step method, as detailed in this book, to invest a small portion of your active income to generate passive income. Over a long period of time, this passive income enables you to become a millionaire or a multi-millionaire: Let's call this the 5th pathway of becoming a millionaire or a multi-millionaire, a pathway that is available to any of us and with almost guaranteed success if you act on it properly and follow it patiently:

(5) You could become a millionaire or a multi-millionaire by following an easy 3-step method as detailed in this book.

This is the essence of this book: an easy 3-step method to help you to invest a portion of your active income to generate passive income to become a millionaire or a multi-millionaire.

The following is a summary of these 3 steps:

Step 1: Mentality: Set your mind to it to become a (multi-) millionaire.

Even though virtually everyone can become a millionaire, if you do not believe in yourself, then nothing good is going to happen! Therefore, it is important to set your mind to it! Maybe writing it down that you can become a millionaire or multi-millionaire somewhere (on a piece of paper, on your phone, on your computer, etc.). Writing it down helps you to internalize an image of becoming a millionaire or multi-millionaire. I know that you can do it once you have set your mind to it!

Then, Step 2 and Step 3 will help you to understand what it takes for you to do differently between becoming a millionaire and becoming a multi-millionaire.

Step 2: Methodology: the method that could enable you to become a millionaire or a multi-millionaire.

We all know the saying that "Knowledge is Money". You may think or fear that only highly educated people with sophisticated knowledge can understand the methodology of becoming a millionaire or a multi-millionaire. And you may think or fear that the methodology must be complicated. Let me tell you right now that this method is extremely simple, virtually anyone with some basic knowledge of elementary school math can easily understand it. This method is simply based on the "magic of the compounding" from Rule of 72. This step (step 2) will show you this "magic" and what this "magic" can do for you if you decide to follow it through with proper actions.

Step 2a: the Rule of 72: the simple math behind this method.
Step 2b: The "magic of the compounding" and "Time is money."

The Rule of 72 is the simple math behind this methodology. Its "magic of the compounding" from the Rule of 72 is discussed in this step.

We all know the saying that "Time is Money". However, what exactly does it mean "Time is money"? The Rule of 72 we are discussing here will give us a clear perspective on how money can grow over time.

The Rule of 72 is a simple math equation that can be used to estimate how long or how many years does it takes to double your money, from $1 to

$2 based on compounding growth, and then from $2 to $4, and from $4 to $8, so on and so forth. It is incredibly simple, and it is "magic" in its power to double your money repeatedly until you are a millionaire or a multi-millionaire, if followed properly.

If it is so simple, why doesn't everyone already know it? And why hasn't everyone already used it to become a millionaire or a multi-millionaire? When I first discovered the Rule of 72, I started to ask around to see if the Rule of 72 is common knowledge to everyone. To my surprise, only an extremely low percentage of the people have heard about the Rule of 72 when I asked them.

In hindsight, this should not be a surprise. The Rule of 72 is not taught in school. Even though I spent 20 years in school until I got my Ph.D. degree, I did not discover the Rule of 72 through school education. I discovered the Rule of 72 through self-learning. And I did not discover the Rule of 72 until I was almost 30 years old. I think that more people will be better off financially if this Rule of 72 becomes known by more people and starts to harvest its "magic" compounding power. This is one of the main reasons why I am detailing my discovery in this book.

One of my regrets is that I did not know the Rule of 72 until I was about 30 years old. And after discovering the Rule of 72, I did not really realize the power of this easy 3-step approach based on the Rule of 72 until many years later, and I did not use it to build wealth earlier.

I hope by sharing my knowledge with you in this book, more people will be made aware of the Rule of 72, and more people will truly appreciate the meaning of "time is money" from the "magic" power of compounding over many years based on the Rule of 72, to help more people like you to become millionaires or multi-millionaires.

Step 2c: The importance of APR in the Rule of 72

To appreciate the true impact of Annual Percentage Rate of return (APR), it is important to understand the following four aspects of the APR and how it will impact your journey to become a millionaire or a multi-millionaire.

(1) The positive impact of APR. A theoretical simulation discusses how fast your money will grow or how many years does it takes to double your money.

(2) The negative impact of APR (for example, in the form of annual interest rate)

(3) Theoretical simulation vs. reality, the average realistic APR (based on historical data)

(4) Instant gratification vs. delayed but much greater gratification

Step 3: Actionality: to act on this method to become a millionaire or a multi-millionaire.

Now we understand the method detailed in step 2 with the "magic" power of the compounding growth based on the Rule of 72, and we also have a realistic expectation of APR based on historical data, step 3 explains how we can harvest this "magic" power to help each one of us to double our money repeatedly and therefore become a millionaire or a multi-millionaire.

As detailed in this step (step 3), using a historically realistic APR, the Rule of 72 can estimate how long it takes to become a millionaire or millionaire. Readers of this book are certainly from different age groups and may have different amounts of money that can be earmarked for long-term investment. To put this in perspective for you, this step dives further into details using an age-based method. This age-based method will show us how long and/or how much money is needed to help either yourself and/or your loved ones to become a millionaire or a multi-millionaire. It will show clearly that the earlier to start your journey, the faster or the easier it is to become a millionaire or a multi-millionaire.

After reading step 3, you can then decide what is your most relevant situation in terms of your age group and money available for investment. Then the most important action is to simply do it!

Step 1: MENTALITY: Set your mind to become a millionaire!

Many years ago, in a house in a small town, a baby was turning one-year young, and a joyful birthday celebration was going on. A few items were placed randomly on the floor: a pencil and a piece of paper, some candies, a few cooked meat and veritable dishes, a new toy, and a new pair of shoes. The mother placed the baby in front of these few items and asked the baby to point to one or to pick one up. The baby looked around and crawled towards the pencil and paper! Everyone laughed and said this baby is going to be a good student and will have a bright future!

That baby was me. My parents did not have much education, not even had opportunities to finish elementary school, but they were incredibly supportive of my education. I was so grateful for their support and went on until I finished my Ph.D. I did not know, when I was a baby, I had set my mind to learning.

After I finished my Ph.D. and my postdoctoral research, I started to work an industry job and with paychecks as my only income. We all know that a job is not guaranteed for life. I always have a sense of insecurity financially. Therefore, I devoted countless hours to studying personal investment. I discovered this incredibly easy method of building wealth overtime by taking advantage of the "Rule of 72". Through this easy 3-step method as detailed in this book, I have built wealth slowly over time and now have a sense of relief financially.

As I mentioned in the introduction, I am surprised and sad that only a small percentage of the people are millionaires here in the USA, because virtually everyone could become a millionaire or even a multi-millionaire based on my own experience and this easy-to-follow 3-step method as detailed in this book.

So, I was asking myself, why aren't there more millionaires, especially if it is so easy? Is it because people naturally prefer instant gratification over delayed gratification? Is it because not enough people are aware of this easy-to-follow 3-step method? I know I certainly do not necessarily have the complete answers to these questions, but I am determined to share my learnings and my knowledge and hope it will be helpful to you.

Now it is your turn to set your mind on it. Where are you now financially and where do you want to be in the future? Since you are reading this book about becoming a millionaire or even a multi-millionaire, then asking yourself, "do I want to become a millionaire or even a multi-millionaire?" "Do I believe in myself that I can become a millionaire or even a multi-millionaire?" I hope your answer is astoundingly YES!

If your answer is YES, then write it down somewhere, on a piece of paper, or on your phone, or on your computer, etc. For example, you can write something like this: "I can (or want to) become a millionaire or even a multi-millionaire" or "I can (or want to) help my loved ones to become a millionaire or even a multi-millionaire." Based on studies by many psychologists, when people write down their goals, instead of just having them vaguely in their thoughts, they are much more successful in achieving the goals than those who did not write down their goals.

Then the rest is easy: by following step 2 and step 3 on how to become a millionaire or even a multi-millionaire.

Let us dive into Step 2: Methodology: the method that will enable you to become a (multi-) millionaire.

Step 2: METHODOLOGY: the method to make you a millionaire.

We all know the saying that "Knowledge is Money." "Rule of 72" is the knowledge we need! In other words, understanding the Rule of 72 and its "magic" power to help your money to make more money for you is the methodology that will enable you to become a millionaire or a multi-millionaire.

Do you know what is 'the Rule of 72"? If your answer is "no", you are not alone. In a recent meeting with a group of more than 30 people of different ages, including many highly educated individuals with Ph.D. degrees, I asked the group if they had heard about "the Rule of 72". I was shocked that only two people knew this rule. Apparently, the Rule of 72 was not taught in schools.

Would you like to know "what is the Rule of 72"?

Would you like to know how you may benefit from this knowledge to make more money?

Would you like to make millions for yourself, and/or for your partner, and/or for your children?

If you answer "yes" to any of these questions, then you owe it to yourself to learn the Rule of 72 and put it in use.

Read on and "Rule on"!

Step 2a: The Rule of 72: the simple math behind this method

What is the Rule of 72?

In investment, the Rule of 72 is a method for estimating how long (how many years) it will take to double your money. The number **72** is divided by the Annual Percentage Rate (APR) of return to obtain the approximate number of years needed for doubling your money:

Approximate years to double your money = 72 / APR.

Table 1. The Rule of 72: Approximate years to double your money, estimated based on the APR. *Please note this is an estimation. More accurate calculation (especially with low or high APR as indicated by *) will be discussed in Step 2b: The importance of annual Percentage Rate (APR) in the Rule of 72).*

The APR of return	Calculation	Approximate years to double your money
1%	72/1 = 72	72*
2%	72/2 =36	36*
6%	72/6 = 12	12*
7.20%	72/7.2 = 10	10
10%	72/10 =7.2	7.2
20%	72/20 =3.6	3.6*

As you can see, for investment, the higher the APR of return, the smaller number of years it will take to double your money. If the APR is 1%, 2%, 6%, 7.2%, 10% or 20%, it will take about 72, 36, 12, 10, 7.2 or 3.6 years to double your money, respectively.

Step 2b: The "magic of compounding" and "Time is money."

This step will explain the magic of compounding from the Rule of 72 that can double your money repeatedly and can grow your money exponentially if invested for a very long time.

Based on the Rule of 72, if the APR=10%, it will take about 7.2 years to double your money (e.g., from $1 to $2). Here are the details on how does $1 grows to $2 over the 7.2 years (See also Table 2).

After 1 year of 10% return, $1 earned $0.1 and became $1.10.
After year 2 of 10% return, $1.1 earned $0.11 and became $1.21.
After year 3 of 10% return, $1.21 earned $0.12 and became $1.33.
After year 4 of 10% return, $1.33 earned $0.13 and became $1.46.
After year 5 of 10% return, $1.46 earned $0.15 and became $1.61.
After year 6 of 10% return, $1.61 earned $0.16 and became $1.77.
After year 7 of 10% return, $1.77 earned $0.177 and became $1.95.
After year 8 of 10% return, $1.95 earned $0.195 and became $2.14.
It reaches $2 after about 7.2 years.

Table 2. Compounding growth of $1 over the years (if the APR is 10%)

After years	$	Accumulated capital gain	Accumulated rate of return
0	Starting with $1		
1	$1.10	$0.10	10%
2	$1.21	$0.21	21%
3	$1.33	$0.33	33%
4	$1.46	$0.46	46%
5	$1.61	$0.61	61%
6	$1.77	$0.77	77%
7	$1.95	$0.95	95%
8	$2.14	$1.14	114%

- The initial $1 invested in this example is called principal or principal capital, the $0.1 gained after year one is interest or capital gain.
- Starting from year 2, both the original principal of $1 from year 0 and interest or capital gain of $0.1 from year 1 starts to earn 10% annual return. Therefore, the new principal is now $1.1. With a 10% return on $1.1, the value increases to $1.21 (=1.1x1.1) after year 2.
- Starting from year 3, both the original principal of $1 and or capital gain of $0.21 accumulated from year 1 and year 2 start to earn 10% annual return. Therefore, the new principal is now $1.21. With a 10% return on $1.21, the value increases to $1.33 (=2.21x1.1) after year 3.
- This process continues over the years, as detailed in table 2, an investment of $1 will double from $1 to $2 after about 7.2 years if the rate of return is 10%

This process of investment value increase over the years from both the original invested principal and accumulated interest or capital gain is referred to as **Compounding**. In other words, compounding is the process where the value of an investment increases because both the principal and accumulated interest or capital gains continue to earn additional interest or capital gain as time passes.

Compounding is a powerful and magical force. Rumor has it that Albert Einstein once said, "Compounding is the 8th wonder of the world. Those who understands it, make money on it … those who do not… lose money on it." It does not matter whether Einstein said those words or not, the truth is that the compounding can work for you (e.g., in investment) or work against you (e.g., in debt payment).

Understanding how compounding works and knowing how to take advantage of it might be your new superpower: you can use it to work for you in investing to help to grow your money. On the flipside, not understanding it could mean that you may end up paying a lot of money in interest for a debt (e.g., credit card debt or mortgage, etc.). More on this in Step 2c.

We all know the saying that Time is money. This is true in the world of investment and is clearly illustrated in Table 3, where the magic of growth through compounding is tabulated up to 80 years. With a 10% rate of return, an investment of $1 will double to $2 after about 7.2 years. Then $2 will double gain in another 7.2 years and becomes $4. $4 will then double to $8. And so on and so forth.

As listed in Table 3, $1 invested for 50 years will grow to $117. $1 invested for 73 years to $1,051. $1 invested for 80 years to $2,048. In other words, $1,000 invested for 73 years or 80 years will reach over 1 million dollars or over 2 million dollars. That is the magic of compounding growth!

Table 3. Compounding growth of $1 over 80 years with APR=10%. Additional details on each year can be found in Appendix #1

After years	Value ($)	Accumulated capital gain ($)	Accumulated rate of return %
0	$1		
1	$1.10	$0.10	10%
7	$1.95	$0.95	95%
8	$2.14	$1.14	114%
10	$2.59	$1.59	159%
20	$6.73	$5.73	573%
30	$17.45	$16.45	1645%
40	$45.26	$44.26	44,26%
50	$117.39	$116.39	11639%
60	$304.48	$303.48	30348%
72	$955.59	$954.59	95459%
73	$1,051.15	$1,050.15	105015%
80	$2,048.40	$2,047.40	204740%

The magic of compounded growth can also be illustrated in Figure 1, where $1 grows to about $117 after invested for 50 years. $1 grows to about $1051 after investing for 73 years. And $1 grows to about $2048 when invested for 80 years.

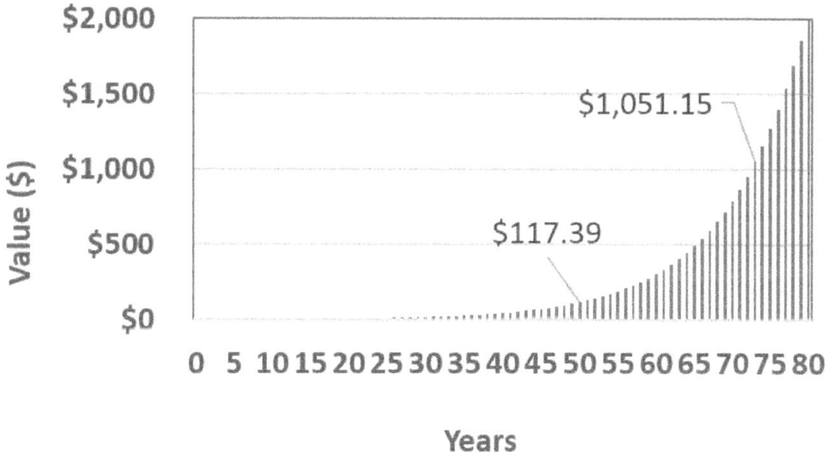

Figure 1. Value of $1 when compounded over 80 years with APR=10%

In summary, the power of compounding growth based on the Rule of 72 has shown us the potential of investing $1,000 as one-time investment to make you a millionaire after 72-73 years. And after another 7 to 8 years (of after 80 years total), these one million dollars will double to 2 million dollars.

72 or 80 years is an exceptionally long time! In real life, we may or may not be able to invest for 72 or 80 years. In step 3, we will discuss how this magic power of compounding can be used for different age groups to become a (multi-) millionaire, without necessarily having to wait for so many years.

However, before going further, we need to have a deeper understanding of the impact of APR, as detailed in Step 2c.

Step 2c: The importance of Annual Percentage Rate (APR)

As discussed in step 2a, the approximate years to double your money can be estimated by a simple formula: 72 / APR. Obviously the higher the APR, the smaller number of years or the faster it is to double your money: this is a positive impact of the APR. The same formula is also applicable when dealing with debt (such as credit card debt). The higher the APR (in the form of annual interest rate), the less numbers of years to double your payment: this is a negative impact of APR. In this step, we will dig deeper into the positive impact and negative impact of APR, then will discuss the realistic APR based on historical data.

(1) The Positive Impact of APR, a mathematical simulation of how APR may impact your investment return.

In general, the higher the APR, the faster it is to double your money.

The simple formula of 72/APR is an approximation from:

$T = \ln(2)/\ln(1+APR/100) \simeq 72/APR$

where:

T = Time (years) to double

Ln = Natural log function

APR = Annual Percentage Rate of return

The Rule of 72 based on this simple formula of 72/APR works very well for APR from 6% to 10%. When the APR is outside the 6%-10% range, an adjustment is usually made to make the estimation more correct. This is done by adding or subtracting 1 from 72 for every 3 points the interest rate diverges from the 8% threshold.

For example:

• If the APR is 1%, it is 7 percentage points lower than 8%, therefore it will mean subtracting 2.3 (for the 6 points lower than 8%) from 72 to lead to the Rule of 69.7.

• If the APR is 5%, it is 3 percentage points lower than 8%, therefore it will mean subtracting 1 (for the 3 points lower than 8%) from 72 to lead to the Rule of 71.

• If the APR is 11%, it is 3 percentage points higher than 8%, therefore adding 1 (for the 3 points higher than 8%) to 72 leads to using the Rule of 73 for more accurate estimation.

• For APR 14%, it would be the rule of 74 (adding 2 for 6 percentage points higher than 8%)

• For APR 23%, it would be the rule of 77 (adding 5 for 15 percentage points higher than 8%)

Let's discuss now the impact if the APR is from 1% to 25%, if making one time investment of $1 or $1,000

As seen in table 4, if APR=1%, it will take about 69.7 years to double from $1 to $2. If investing $1,000, it will reach over one million ($1,024,000) after 697 years (more details in table 4). Obviously, APR=1% is too low for generating meaningful investment return

If APR=8%, it will take about 9 years to double from $1 to $2. The $2 will double to $4 after another 9 years (18 years total). And it will reach $1024 after "double" 10 times (or after 90 years). If investing $1,000, it will reach over one million ($1,024,000) after 90 years.

If APR=10%, it will take about 7.2 years to double from $1 to $2. The $2 will double to $4 after another 7.2 years (14.4 years total). And it will reach $1024 after "double" 10 times (or after 72.7 years). If investing $1,000, it will reach over one million ($1,024,000) after 72.7 years.

If APR=12%, it will take about 6.1 years to double from $1 to $2. The $2 will double to $4 after another 6.1 years (12.2 years total). And it will reach $1024 after "double" 10 times (or after 61.1 years). If investing $1,000, it will reach over one million ($1,024,000) after about 61.1 years.

Table 4. The Impact of APR. The higher the APR, the faster it is to double your money. Initial investment of $1 or $1000 ($1k). The $ amount and years to double are approximations and are for illustration purposes only.

Balance ($)		**Years**				
		if APR 1%	**if APR 8%**	**if APR 10%**	**if APR 12%**	**if APR 25%**
$1	$1k	0	0	0	0	0
$2	$2k	69.7	9	7.2	6.1	3.1
$4	$4k	139.4	18	14.4	12.2	6.2
$8	$8k	209.1	27	21.6	18.3	9.3
$16	$16k	278.8	36	28.8	24.4	12.4
$32	$32k	348.5	45	36	30.6	15.5
$64	$64k	418.2	54	43.2	36.7	18.6
$128	$128k	487.9	63	50.4	42.8	21.7
$256	$256k	557.6	72	57.6	48.9	24.9
$512	$512k	627.3	81	64.8	55	28
$1,024	$1,024k	697	90	72.7	61.1	31.1
$2,048	$2,048k	766.7	99	80	67.2	34.2

If APR=15%, it will take about 5 years to double from $1 to $2. The $2 will double to $4 after another 5 years (10 years total). And it will reach $1024 after "double" 10 times (or after 50 years). If investing $1,000, it will reach over one million ($1,024,000) after 49.6 years.

If APR=25%, it will take about 3.1 years to double from $1 to $2. The $2 will double to $4 after another 3.1 years (6.2 years total). And it will reach $1024 after "double" 10 times (or after 31 years). If investing $1,000, it will reach over one million ($1,024,000) after 31.1 years.

Once the balance reaches one million dollars, the next double will take it to 2 million dollars, and the next double of 2 million dollars will take it to 4 million dollars, so on and so forth.

Another way to appreciate the enormous impact of APR is to look at the huge gap of end balance among different APRs, as seen in Table 5.

Table 5. Balance ($) for $1,000 invested for 10 to 60 years, APR =1% to 25%

APR	1%	8%	10%	12%	15%	25%
$ year 0	$1,000	$1,000	$1,000	$1,000	$1,000	$1,000
$ 10 years	$1,105	$2,159	$2,594	$3,106	$4,046	$9,313
$ 20 years	$1,220	$4,661	$6,727	$9,646	$16,367	$86,736
$ 30 years	$1,348	$10,063	$17,449	$29,960	$66,212	$807,793
$ 40 years	$1,489	$21,724	$45,259	$93,051	$267,864	$7,523,163
$ 50 years	$1,644	$46,902	$117,391	$289,002	$1,083,657	$70,064,923
$ 60 years	$1,817	$101,257	$304,482	$897,596	$4,383,999	$652,530,447

If APR=1%, after 60 years, $1,000 only grows to $1817.

If APR=8%, after 60 years, $1,000 grows to $101,257.

If APR=10%, after 60 years, $1,000 grows to $304,482.

If APR=12%, after 60 years, $1,000 grows to $897,596.

If APR=15%, after 60 years, $1,000 grows to $4,383,999 (>4 million $).

In the unlikely scenario of consistent APR=25% for many years, after 40 years, $1,000 grows to $7,523,163 which is more than 7 million dollars! Then after 60 years, $1,000 grows to $652,530,447 which is more than 652 million dollars! Since at 25%, it takes just 3.1 years to double your money, then after another 3.1 years (or 63 years total), the initial $1,000 is now $1,305,060,894, which is over one billion dollars! Incredible, isn't it?

A 10% difference in APR (from 15% to 25%), when compound for many years, makes a dramatic difference between millionaire and billionaire!

You may say this is too good to be true. To a certain extent, it is too good to be true in the sense that it is almost impossible to have a very high APR (for example 25%) consistently over many years. However, the good news is that there is no need to have such a high APR to become a millionaire or a multi-millionaire, as will be discussed in Step 2c, section (3) when we review over 90 years of historical data.

(2): The Negative impact of APR (in the form of annual interest rate)

The magic of compounding based on the Rule of 72 was clearly shown from the examples in Step 2c, section (1). In terms of creating wealth by investment, the higher APR, the better.

Unfortunately, the magic of compounding based on the Rule of 72 could also impact the living cost (or expense) of our daily life. The APR related to our daily life may be presented in different forms, such as interest rate for debt payments, or inflation rate that affects the purchasing power of our money. Debt may come in many forms, including credit det debt and various loans (car loan, student loan, mortgages., etc.).

As opposite to investment where the higher possible APR, the better, for any expense items related to our daily life, the lower the APR (or the interest rate or the inflation rate), the better. In this section, we will discuss how to leverage our knowledge of the Rule of 72, to minimize the negative impact and to harvest the positive impact of APR to our life, with the goal of increasing our net worth (net worth = income – expense).

To avoid credit card debt

Based on most recent data from the survey by the U.S. Federal Reserve, the average credit card debt of U.S. households is approximately $5,700. This is terrible. To become a millionaire, one must do everything possible to avoid debt. If already in debt, one must pay off the debt before starting investing. This is because it is a double-edged saw: the wonderful Rule of the 72 that can help you to increase your net worth or even to become a millionaire by compounding your investment gain, will also compound the interest you owed to a lender, which will quickly make you to owe much more money or into having more debt, as discussed in the example below (Table 6).

Table 6. The Rule of 72 is now working against you, when applied to debts (17% APR)

After years	Amount Owed ($)	Accumulated Interest ($)	Accumulated rate of cost %	Amount Owed ($)
0	$1			$1,000
1	$1.17	$0.17	17%	$1,170
2	$1.37	$0.37	37%	$1,369
3	$1.60	$0.60	60%	$1,602
4	$1.87	$0.87	87%	$1,874
5	$2.19	$1.19	119%	$2,192
6	$2.57	$1.57	157%	$2,565
7	$3.00	$2.00	200%	$3,001
8	$3.51	$2.51	251%	$3,511
9	$4.11	$3.11	311%	$4,108
10	$4.81	$3.81	381%	$4,807
11	$5.62	$4.62	462%	$5,624

According to the survey by the Federal Reserve, the average Annual Percentage Rate (APR) charged for credit card accounts is ~17%! This horribly high APR will double the amount of money you owed to the lender in just about 4.4 years!

With 17% APR, if you owe $1,000 and don't make any payment, you may owe $1874 after 4 years, $2192 after 5 years, and $4807 after 10 years.

Unfortunately, many of the credit cards have an even higher APR.

Table 7 is an example with 25% APR, if you owe $1,000 and don't make any payment, you may owe $1953 just after 3 years, $3052 after 5 years, and $9313 after 10 years. Clearly a financial disaster if owing such a high interest credit card!

With the borrowing and spending culture here in the USA, there are even people who got into credit card debt to take vacations. Depending on your credit card interest rate and if you cannot pay it off quickly, the actual vacation cost can be much higher than the original amount spent during the vacation. This is not a wise financial decision.

The only solution is to either not use a credit card or to pay off the balance each month to avoid any late charge and interest payment.

Table 7. The Rule of 72 is now working against you, when applied to debts (25% APR)

After years	**Amount Owed ($)**	**Accumulated Interest ($)**	**Accumulated rate of cost %**	**Amount Owed ($)**
0	$1			$1,000
1	$1.25	$0.25	25%	$1,250
2	$1.56	$0.31	56%	$1,563
3	$1.95	$0.39	95%	$1,953
4	$2.44	$0.49	144%	$2,441
5	$3.05	$0.61	205%	$3,052
6	$3.81	$0.76	281%	$3,815
7	$4.77	$0.95	377%	$4,768
8	$5.96	$1.19	496%	$5,960
9	$7.45	$1.49	645%	$7,451
10	$9.31	$1.86	831%	$9,313
11	$11.64	$2.33	1064%	$11,642

To minimize mortgage debt

It is common that we have mortgage debt at some time point of our life. In addition to shopping for a mortgage with the lowest possible interest rate, if you can afford the higher monthly payment from a 15-year mortgage, try to stay with a 15-year mortgage, not a 30-year mortgage. This is mainly for two reasons: (1) APR is higher for a 30-year mortgage than for a 15-year mortgage, (2) the wonderful Rule of 72 works against you with higher interest payment when compounded for 30 years than for 15 years.

In the hypothetical examples below (Table 8), for a $300,000 loan, one would save $79,235 to $115,054 if going with 15-year mortgage (assuming the APRs are 2% to 3.5% in Table 8, if the APRs are different, then the saving will be different). In addition, you will also have a peace of mind of paying off the mortgage 15 years sooner.

Table 8. Saving estimation for 15-year mortgage vs. 30-year mortgage. Monthly payment did not include property tax, etc. Note that this table for illustration was done before the Federal reserve increase the increase rate. The saving will be higher if the difference mortgage rate increases between a 15-year mortgage and a 30-year mortgage.

Mortgage	**Loan amount ($)**	**APR**	**Monthly payment ($)**	**Total interest ($)**	Total payment ($)
30 years	$300,000	2.5%	$1,185	$126,730	$426,730
15 years	$300,000	2.0%	$1,931	$47,495	$347,495
Estimated saving: $79,235					
Mortgage	Loan amount ($)	APR	Monthly payment ($)	Total interest ($)	Total payment ($)
30 years	$300,000	3.5%	$1,347	$184,968	$484,968
15 years	$300,000	3.0%	$2,072	$72,914	$372,914
Estimated saving: $115,054					

Student loans

Besides housing cost or mortgage, education is another huge expense item. However, there are many options to tackle education expenses.

The cost of 4-year undergraduate tuition varies so much, it can be essentially free, for example, if going to an in-state public university that offers generous and relatively easy to get scholarships, or it can be as high as $200,000 to $250,000 if going to an expensive private school. If you are getting a full ride from financial aid or from a scholarship or from a rich family, then enjoy the private schools. However, if you must take out a student loan to go to an expensive school, then it is best to stay with an affordable school to avoid a student loan, with two obvious benefits:

- A peace of mind of not having to worry about repayment your student loan over the next 10 to 20 years.
- Considering this as a saved opportunity cost: Whatever amount you effectively saved without a student loan will help you to become a millionaire so much faster, as compared if you were to take out a student loan). For example, $50,000 saved and invested for 32 years with an APR=10% will get about $1.05 million. And $250,000 saved and invested for just 15 years in APR=10% will get about $1.04 million.

Table 9. Student loan repayment examples. The loan amount and APR are hypothetical.

Loan amount	Term (years)	APR	Monthly payment	Total interest	Total payment
$250,000	10	5%	$2,652	$68,240	$318,240
	20	5%	$1,650	$146,000	$396,000
	10	4%	$2,531	$53,720	$303,720
	20	4%	$1,515	$113,600	$363,600
$50,000	10	5%	$530	$13,600	$63,600
	20	5%	$330	$29,200	$79,200
	10	4%	$506	$10,720	$60,720
	20	4%	$303	$22,720	$72,720

Inflation.

Inflation is a financial term describing the increase in prices of goods and services within a period, for example, per year. Inflation reduces the purchasing power of our money. The higher the inflation rate, the less the purchasing power. The inflation rate over the years in the USA is listed in Table 10. From 1961 to 2020, the inflation rate fluctuates widely. And we all know the inflation rate was extremely high for 2022.

Table 10. Inflation rate over the years (up to 2020) in the USA

Year	Inflation Rate (%)	Year	Inflation Rate (%)	Year	Inflation Rate (%)
1961	1.1	1981	10.3	2001	2.8
1962	1.2	1982	6.1	2002	1.6
1963	1.2	1983	3.2	2003	2.3
1964	1.3	1984	4.3	2004	2.7
1965	1.6	1985	3.5	2005	3.4
1966	3	1986	1.9	2006	3.2
1967	2.8	1987	3.7	2007	2.9
1968	4.3	1988	4.1	2008	3.8
1969	5.5	1989	4.8	2009	-0.4
1970	5.8	1990	5.4	2010	1.6
1971	4.3	1991	4.2	2011	3.2
1972	3.3	1992	3	2012	2.1
1973	6.2	1993	3	2013	1.5
1974	11.1	1994	2.6	2014	1.6
1975	9.1	1995	2.8	2015	0.1
1976	5.7	1996	2.9	2016	1.3
1977	6.5	1997	2.3	2017	2.1
1978	7.6	1998	1.6	2018	2.4
1979	11.3	1999	2.2	2019	1.8
1980	13.5	2,000	3.4	2020	1.2

(3): Simulation vs. reality, the average realistic APR (based on historical data)

The simulation in Step 2c, section (1) deviates from the reality of investment world mainly in following aspects:

#1: It assumes that the investment is held for an exceptionally long time. In the real world, not everyone will have the patience or stamina to be an investor (means holding the investment for many years). Some people will become traders who may cash out an investment after a brief period, e.g., a few days, a few months, or a few years, and therefore the investment does not have enough time to benefit from the magic of exponential compounding growth.

#2: It assumes consistent APR each year, in real-world the APR fluctuates each year.

#3: It assumes positive APR (or APR>0%) each year, in real-world the APR can also be negative (<0%) or severely negatively (well below 0%), although the APR is positive 70% of time (or 2 years out of every 3 years) over a long period, based on historical data.

#4: The simulation for investment return using consistent high APR (e.g., 15% or 25%) over long periods of time could be too good to be true, because it is not possible to have such a consistent high APR over long periods of time (e.g., over 60 years as in table 4 and table 5). However, it is possible to have such a high APR over certain years, for example, historical S&P 500 index data has logged APR>25% for 24 years out of 93 years, and APR>15% for 45 years out of 93 years.

So, what is a realistic APR based on historical stock market data? There are thousands of stocks trading on U.S. stock exchanges. When people say, "the stock market," Vanguard Total Stock Market Index Fund (ticker: VTSAX) is often cited as a good proxy. VTSAX had an APR of about 14% for the last 10 years. However, VTSAX has only about 20 years of historical data that I can find and therefore, it is not necessarily a good proxy for the whole stock market that has been in existence much longer than 20 years.

The S&P 500 is a collection of 500 of the largest publicly traded U.S. companies. The list of the 500 companies may be updated quarterly and annually. The S&P 500 index makes up about 80% of the entire stock market value and has a long track record. Therefore, the S&P 500 Index is often used as a good proxy to benchmark the performance of the whole stock market.

In the previous sections, we used APR=10% for investment return simulation based on the Rule of 72. In this section, let us dig deeper into the historical stock market return data to see if 10% is a reasonable APR?

I downloaded the historical annual return data of S&P 500 from 1928 to 2022. There are two sets of data available: the total return of S&P 500 index, as shown as APR with dividend in Table 11, or the return from price appreciation only (excluding the contribution from dividend), as shown as APR excluding dividend. Dividends are payments made by publicly traded companies to eligible shareholders as a reward to investors for investing their money into the companies. Dividends may be paid monthly, quarterly, or yearly. Not all public traded companies pay a dividend. Of its five-hundred-member companies in the S&P 500 index, 84% of the companies pay dividends.

As seen from Table 11, the APR varies widely from as low as -43% to as high as 53% (also shown in Figure 2) and more than 70% of the years the APR is above 0%. Even after the terrible year of 2022, the overall average APR with dividend for the last 95 years (from 1928 to 2022) is 11.71%. The overall average APR excluding dividend for the last 95 years (from 1928 to 2022) is 7.72%. Therefore, 10% is reasonable as APR in our earlier simulations.

Table 11 (see next page). APR of S&P 500 index. APR (a) is the APR with dividend and APR (b) is APR excluding dividend. The overall average APR for the last 93 years (from year 1928 to 2020) is 11.89% with dividend and 7.78% excluding dividend, respectively. We know that the Stock market had a wonderful year in 2021 with 28.41% return for S&P 500 index but had a terrible year in 2022 with 18.32% loss. The overall average APR for the last 95 years (from year 1928 to 2022) is 11.71% with dividend and 7.72% excluding dividend, respectively.

Table 11 APR of S&P 500 index. APR (a) is the APR with dividend and APR (b) is APR excluding dividend.

Year	APR (a)	APR (b)	Year	APR (a)	APR (b)	Year	APR (a)	APR (b)
2022	-18.30%	-19.80%	1990	-3.10%	-6.60%	1958	43.40%	38.10%
2021	28.40%	26.60%	1989	31.70%	27.30%	1957	-10.80%	-14.30%
2020	18.40%	16.30%	1988	16.60%	12.40%	1956	6.60%	2.60%
2019	31.50%	28.90%	1987	5.30%	2.00%	1955	31.60%	26.40%
2018	-4.40%	-6.20%	1986	18.70%	14.60%	1954	52.60%	45.00%
2017	21.80%	19.40%	1985	31.70%	26.30%	1953	-1.00%	-6.60%
2016	12.00%	9.50%	1984	6.30%	1.40%	1952	18.40%	11.80%
2015	1.40%	-0.70%	1983	22.60%	17.30%	1951	24.00%	16.50%
2014	13.70%	11.40%	1982	21.60%	14.80%	1950	31.70%	21.80%
2013	32.40%	29.60%	1981	-4.90%	-9.70%	1949	18.80%	10.30%
2012	16.00%	13.40%	1980	32.40%	25.80%	1948	5.50%	-0.70%
2011	2.10%	0.00%	1979	18.40%	12.30%	1947	5.70%	0.00%
2010	15.10%	12.80%	1978	6.60%	1.10%	1946	-8.10%	-11.90%
2009	26.50%	23.50%	1977	-7.20%	-11.50%	1945	36.40%	30.70%
2008	-37.00%	-38.50%	1976	23.80%	19.20%	1944	19.80%	13.80%
2007	5.50%	3.50%	1975	37.20%	31.60%	1943	25.90%	19.50%
2006	15.80%	13.60%	1974	-26.50%	-29.70%	1942	20.30%	12.40%
2005	4.90%	3.00%	1973	-14.70%	-17.40%	1941	-11.60%	-17.90%
2004	10.90%	9.00%	1972	19.00%	15.60%	1940	-9.80%	-15.30%
2003	28.70%	26.40%	1971	14.30%	10.80%	1939	-0.40%	-5.50%
2002	-22.10%	-23.40%	1970	4.00%	0.10%	1938	31.10%	25.20%
2001	-11.90%	-13.00%	1969	-8.50%	-11.40%	1937	-35.00%	-38.60%
2,000	-9.10%	-10.10%	1968	11.10%	7.70%	1936	33.90%	27.90%
1999	21.00%	19.50%	1967	24.00%	20.10%	1935	47.70%	41.40%
1998	28.60%	26.70%	1966	-10.10%	-13.10%	1934	-1.40%	-5.90%
1997	33.40%	31.00%	1965	12.50%	9.10%	1933	54.00%	46.60%
1996	23.00%	20.30%	1964	16.50%	13.00%	1932	-8.20%	-15.20%
1995	37.60%	34.10%	1963	22.80%	18.90%	1931	-43.30%	-47.10%
1994	1.30%	-1.50%	1962	-8.70%	-12.00%	1930	-24.90%	-28.50%
1993	10.10%	7.10%	1961	26.90%	23.10%	1929	-8.40%	-11.90%
1992	7.60%	4.50%	1960	0.50%	-3.00%	1928	43.60%	37.90%
1991	30.50%	26.30%	1959	12.00%	8.50%			

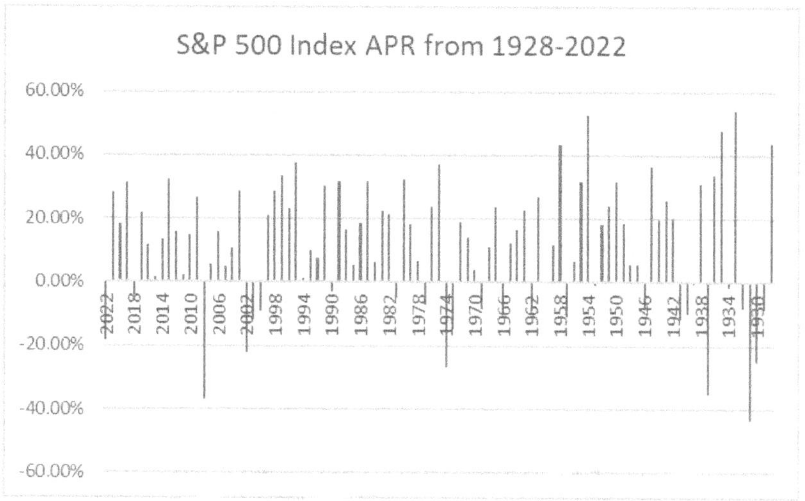

Figure 2: S&P 500 index annual return (including dividend) from 1928 to 2022. If an investment is only held for a short period (e.g., one year or 2 years or less than 5 years), the risk of losing money is very high.

Let's look at the average APR over different periods, from year 2022 and counting backwards to 1928, including 10, 20, 30, 40, 50, 60, 70 and 95 years.

The average APR is remarkably close to 11% to 12% over different periods, even though the APR varies widely from as low as -43% to as high as 53%.

- 13.7% for the most recent 10 years (2013-2022)
- 11.3% for the last 20 years (2003-2022)
- 11.2% for the recent 30 years (1993-2022)
- 12.6% for the last 40 years (1983-2022)
- 11.8% for the last 50 years (1973-2022)
- 11.6 % for the last 60 years (1963-2022)
- 12.1% for the last 70 years (1953-2022)
- and finally, 11.7% for the last 95 years (1928-2022)

(4) Instant gratification vs. delayed but much greater gratification.

If you manage to avoid debt, it is obvious that lowering your expenses (spending less or delaying some spending) will also increase your net worth. It is easier said than done though.

Speaking of spending less, think hard if your spending is "needs" (food, shelter, transportation, medical cost, etc.) or "wants" (fancy food or dining out, luxury car, vacation, etc.).

Speaking of delaying some spending, think twice before you spend money on "wants." Would you rather spend the money on "wants" now for instant gratification? or save the money on "wants" for investment that will give you delayed but potentially much greater gratification?

Here are a few examples:

Example #1: Coffee: $5 or $600 or $5,000 per cup?

Do you spend money on buying fancy coffee occasionally or every day? If you are willing to spend $5 now on a fancy cup of coffee, fine and enjoy it. However, if it is not a $5 a cup coffee, but a $600* or even $5,000** a cup of coffee, would you still buy this cup of coffee now? In other words, the $5 saved and invested could potentially grow to $600 or even $5,000 over the years with the magic of compounding growth. And then you can spend the $600 or even $5,000 for delayed but greater gratifications (for example, many more cups of coffee, or a vacation, etc.)

*: $600 is estimated based on the power of compounding growth: $5 invested for 50.3 years with an APR=10% could grow about 120 folds and turn $5 into about $600.

**: Similarly, $5,000 is based on the estimation that $5 invested for 49.5 years with an APR=15% could grow >1,000 folds and turn $5 into about $5,000.

For following estimation, let us just use APR=10% since APR=10% is realistically achievable and APR=15% is difficult to achieve.

Now if you were to buy a cup of $5 coffee every day, which is $150 a month or $1,800 a year now. This spending of $1,800 per year on coffee, if saved and invested for 50 years at 10% of return, it could lead to $211,303 for a delayed gratification.

If you were to do this for 5 years, it would cost $9,000 to buy coffee. $9,000 saved and invested for 50 years at 10% APR could grow to $1,056,517. This means drinking up more than one-million-dollar of coffee when viewed under the lens of delayed gratification (see Table 12)

It is certainly unrealistic to answer a coffee lover not to drink any coffee. What about making homemade coffee most of the time? If the cost of making one's own coffee is $1 a cup, then this corresponds to a saving of $4 per day, or $120 a month or $1,440 a year. This $1,440 invested over 50 years could grow to $169,042. And for 5 years, the saving will be $7,200. This $7,200 invested for 50 years could grow to $845,214. And for 10 years, the saving will be $14,400. This $14,400 invested over 50 years could grow to $1,690,428.

Table 12. Hypothetical cost of drinking coffee and potential saving in drinking homemade coffee

Examples	Instant gratification	Delayed (~50 years) gratification
Cost of drinking coffee	$5 per cup now	$600
	$150 per month	$18,000
	$1,800 per year	$211,303
	$9,000 (5 years)	$1,056,517
Potential cost saving from homemade coffee	**Potential Saving**	**Delayed (about 50 years) gratification from saving**
	$1,440 (1 year)	$169,042
	$7,200 (5 years)	$845,214
	$14,400 (10 years)	$1,690,428

While this example assumes buying a fancy coffee every day over 5 years or 10 years, which certainly may not be the case. But hopefully the estimation helps to illustrate the opportunity for saving, whether it is buying coffee or other spending, such as dining out.

Example #2: $2,000 vacation or a million-dollar vacation?

Do your family take an annual vacation or even vacations? Have you taken your baby to Disneyland or Disney world? I know I did. When I asked my children if they remembered their 1st trip to Disney and the answer was a solid no!

My children do remember the 2nd trip to Disney when they were teenagers, but not the 1st trip when they were 2 years old. The 1st trip seems a waste of money.

I am certainly not suggesting everyone not taking vacations, but I certainly wish I saved and invested the money instead of taking my baby to a Disney at the age of 2. This example of delayed gratification is clearly shown by the estimation in Table 14 (next page). If I had saved the $2,000 money spent on the trip and invested it in a S&P 500 index fund, there could be a million-dollar waiting there for me or for my baby in the years to come. Or alternatively, if I were to just buy Disney stock instead of the 1st trip about 20 years, when the stock price was about $25 a share, now the Disney stock (DIS) is about $100 a share (early 2023), the $2,000 has already grow to more than 4 folds to >$8,000, it could be even higher if counting in dividend re-investment. And the Disney stock could continue to appreciate in the coming years, and potentially maybe even better than investing in the S&P 500 index fund (please note that this is not a recommendation of buying Disney stock, but as an example to demonstrate the potential benefit of delayed gratification vs. instant gratification).

In summary, understanding how APR may impact our expenses will help us to carefully plan our spending, so we will be able to save more money for our investment journey to increase our net worth and to become a millionaire or a multi-millionaire.

Table 14: Instant gratification ($2,000, one vacation) vs. delayed gratification (possibly a million-dollar or more, for multiple vacations)

Examples	**Instant gratification**	**Delayed gratification**
Family vacation	$1,000	$120,000 **(after 50-51 years)**
		$500,000 **(after 65-66 years)**
	$2,000	$240,000 **(after 50-51 years)**
		$1,000,000 **(after 65-66 years) (a million dollars!)**

Step 3: ACTIONALITY: To act on this method to become a millionaire.

Now we are ready to follow the method to harvest the compounded growth based on Rule of 72.

However, the situation is unique for each of us, in terms of your current situation and expectations.

Current situation:

(1) Wat's your age or age group?
(2) How much money is available for investment?
(3) How long (how many years) can the money be invested?

Expectations:

(1) Do you want to become a millionaire or a multi-millionaire?
(2) How soon do you want to become a millionaire or a multi-millionaire?

While the method detailed in step 2 based the rule of 72 is universal, it needs to be tailored to your unique situation and expectations. In this step, we'll dig deeper into the three of the most important factors related to the Rule of 72 and will present it in an age (or age group)-based approach and you can choose one of them that works best for your situation and expectation.

As already discussed in Step 2, the interdependence of these three factors related to the Rule of 72 will determine how quickly you could become a millionaire or a multi-millionaire.

Factor #1: Money: how much money is available to invest? This is intuitive, the more money that can be invested, the easier or the faster it is to become a millionaire or a multi-millionaire. The key question is: what's the minimum amount of money needed to be invested? The answer to this question depends on Factor #2 below.

Factor #2: Time: how long can the money be invested? As discussed in step 2, the longer the time horizon (e.g., 50, 60, 72 or even 80 years), the less amount of money needs to be invested to become a millionaire or a multi-millionaire. We will discuss how this Time factor relates to different age groups.

Factor #3: Compounding rate: what is the Annual Percentage Rate of return (APR)? The higher the better, as discussed in detail in Step 2. To make it simple and realistic, in this Step 3, we will use historical average of APR=10% to discuss the strategies on how to become a millionaire or a multi-millionaire, based on your age (or age group).

Using APR=10%, we will illustrate how to best take advantage of the inter-dependency between Factor #1 (Money) and Factor #2 (Time) to make you a millionaire or a multi-millionaire. The strategy is sorted based on your age group in combination with one time investment vs re-occurring investments.

Then you can choose one of them that best fits your situation and expectations to start the journey to a millionaire or a multi-millionaire.

As already mentioned, it is extremely simple but needs commitment to long-term investment. One possibility is to simply buy and hold an investment such as S&P 500 index fund* and then sit back and relax, and let the compounded growth do its magic to make you a millionaire or a multi-millionaire.

*: There are many options to invest in S&P 500 index fund, to name just a few, there is SPDR S&P 500 exchange traded fund (ETF) (SPY), or Vanguard S&P 500 ETF (VOO), or Invesco S&P 500 Index Fund (SPIAX), or Fidelity® 500 Index Fund (FXAIX). These funds are similar, whichever to buy would largely depend on your personal preference.

Step 3a: Age group 0 to 1, Baby future millionaires

Let us start with the easiest one: how to make your baby a future millionaire or a multi-millionaire. Step 3a is an excellent strategy for a parent or a grandparent who would like to make their children or grandchildren future millionaires or multi-millionaires.

As already discussed, the longer the money can be invested, the easier it is to become a millionaire.

Therefore, if you are a young couple who is expecting a baby or just had a baby or having a young child, or if you a grandparent and is expecting a grandchild, you could give your baby and/or your grandbaby possibly one of the best birth presents that you can ever give: to easily make you baby or grandbaby a future millionaire or a multi-millionaire, starting with as little as just one time investment of $1,000.

One time investment of $1,000 could make your baby a future millionaire after 72 years. One time investment of $2,000 could make your baby a future millionaire when she or he is 65~66 years old (see Table 15)

Table 15. Make your baby a future millionaire or multi-millionaire, starting with just one time investment of ≥$1,000.

Years	**End balance ($) APR=10%**				
	$1,000 invested	$2,000 invested	$3,000 invested	$4,000 invested	$5,000 invested
10	$2,600	$5,200	$7,800	$10,400	$13,000
20	$6,700	$13,400	$20,100	$26,800	$33,500
30	$17,500	$35,000	$52,500	$70,000	$87,500
40	$45,000	$90,000	$135,000	$180,000	$225,000
50	$117,391	$234,782	$352,173	$469,563	$586,954
55	$189,059	$378,118	$567,177	$756,236	$945,295
60	$304,482	$608,964	$913,446	**$1,217,928**	**$1,522,410**
66	$539,407	**$1,078,814**	**$1,618,221**	**$2,157,628**	**$2,697,035**
73	$1,051,153	$2,102,306	$3,153,460	$4,204,613	$5,255,766
80	$2,048,400	$4,096,800	$6,145,201	$8,193,601	$10,242,001

Considering that the normal retirement age currently is 65 to 67 years old and considering that the average retirement savings for people ages 65-69 in the U.S is only about $200,000 (see next page *in italic font**). **This is fantastic if your baby or grandbaby could become a millionaire or a multi-millionaire at his or her retirement with your one-time birthday gift towards investment.** Please note this birthday gift for investment needs to be held for a long time and no tax implication is discussed here.

It gets even better: A simple one-time investment of $2,000 will make your baby a millionaire when she or he reaches retirement age 66! One time investment of $3,000 could make your baby a future millionaire when she or he is just over 60 years old. One time investment of $4,000 could grow to over 2 million dollars after 66 years, an easy way to make your baby a future multi-millionaire!

After this initial one-time investment, nothing stops you from continuing to invest in your baby, and to teach your baby to continue to invest, to easily become a multi-millionaire.

There has been discussion or suggestion that our government should give each newborn baby a $1,000 gift so each of them can become a millionaire. We know it is not happening from the government side. But you can do it yourself!

To recap, if you have decided to help to make your baby a future millionaire or a multi-millionaire, open a custodial account and start to invest (e.g., buying a S&P 500 index fund or exchange traded fund (ETF)) on your baby's behalf. A one-time birthday gift of $2000 if invested for a very long time (mor than 66 years if with APR of 10%) could potentially be a delayed but an incredible gift or gratification of more than one million dollars for your baby!

And it is possible to help your baby to become a future multi-millionaire if invested more than $2000 initially or with additional investment over the years, as detailed in the remaining sections of step 3.

Please note this means holding an investment for an extremely long time (66 years or more) and no tax implications have been considered here. The exact years of becoming a millionaire or a multi-millionaire may also vary due to market volatility and other risks as discussed in Bonus 1 to 5.

And if a one-time gift of $2000 is not affordable, then there are also ways to spread the $2000 over a few years or over many years, as detailed in step 3b.

** 2019-2020 Federal Reserve SCF (Survey of Consumer Finances) data, the average retirement savings by age in the U.S.:*

- *Ages 18-24: $4,745*
- *Ages 25-29: $9,408*
- *Ages 30-34: $21,731*
- *Ages 35-39: $48,710*
- *Ages 40-44: $101,899*
- *Ages 45-49: $148,950*
- *Ages 50-54: $146,068*
- *Ages 55-59: $223,493*
- *Ages 60-64: $221,451*
- Ages 65-69: $206,819

Step 3b: Age group 0-10, Young child future millionaires

Not every parent may have a lump sum of $1,000 or $2000 to invest when a baby is born. Or you may have the money but did not get a chance to invest. What now? How to make your young child a future millionaire or a multi-millionaire. It is still easy: one can also invest over the years and still make your young child a future millionaire or a multi-millionaire.

Depending on your situation, you can start with a different amount of money and invest for different number of years. The examples below illustrate three scenarios:

#1: To get to over 1 million dollars at age 67 by investing $500 for 4 years ($2,000 total invested), for example, from age 0 to age 4.

#2: If you miss the opportunity to invest for your baby from age 0 to 4, you can still make your baby a millionaire at age 67 by investing $500 for 6 years ($3,000 total invested), for example, from age 5 to age 10.

#3: If you would like to make your baby a multi-millionaire, you could invest $500 for 10 years ($5,000 total invested), for example, from age 0 to age 10. This could be more than 2 million dollars at age 67.

Table 16. Make your baby a millionaire at age 67, starting with $500 year for 4 years ($2,000 total invested). Or help your baby to get to 2 million dollars, starting with $500 year for 10 years ($5,000 total invested). If APR=10%.

Age	$ invested	Years invested	End balance	Total balance	Note
1	$500	67	$296,674	$1,034,459	$2,000 invested, $500 each year at age 1 to 4
2	$500	66	$269,704		
3	$500	65	$245,185		
4	$500	64	$222,896		
5	$500	63	$202,632	$2,005,224	$5,000 invested, $500 each year from age 1 to 10
6	$500	62	$184,211		
7	$500	61	$167,464		
8	$500	60	$152,240		
9	$500	59	$138,400		
10	$500	58	$125,818		

If investing $1,000 per year, it gets better (as shown in Table 17)

Table 17. Make your baby a millionaire at age 67, starting with $1,000 year for 2 years ($2,000 total invested). Or help your baby to get to >2 million dollars, starting with $1,000 year for 4 years ($4,000 total invested). Or for >2 million dollars, starting with $1,000 year for 10 years ($1,0000 total invested). If APR=10% and the investments are held until the age of 67.

0	$ invested	Years invested	End balance	Total balance (at the age of 67)
1	$1,000	67	$593,349	#1: $1,132,757 ($2,000 total invested, $1,000/year, age 1 to 2)
2	$1,000	66	$539,408	
3	$1,000	65	$490,371	
4	$1,000	64	$445,792	#2: $2,068,920 ($4,000 total invested, $1,000/year, age 1 to 4)
5	$1,000	63	$405,264	
6	$1,000	62	$368,422	
7	$1,000	61	$334,928	#3: $4,010,449 ($1,0000 total invested, $1,000/year, age 1 to 10)
8	$1,000	60	$304,480	
9	$1,000	59	$276,800	
10	$1,000	58	$251,636	

Certainly, you don't have to stop at age 10 and can continue to invest more starting from age 11 and to become a multi-millionaire, as discussed below for the other age groups (age 11 and up)

To recap, if you have decided to help to make your young child a future millionaire, open a custodial account and start to invest on your child's behalf. As detailed in table 16 and 17, starting to invest from the age of 1 to 10 (for example, a $500 or $1000 per year, if invested for a very long time (58 years or more if with APR of 10%)) offers many possible scenarios to help your young child to become a millionaire or a multi-millionaire.

Again, please note this means holding an investment for an extremely long time (58 to 67 years) and no tax implications have been considered here. The exact years of becoming a millionaire or a multi-millionaire may also vary due to market volatility and other risks as detailed in Bonus 1 to 5.

Step 3c: Age 11 to 20: "Teenager" future millionaires

"Teenager" is usually a person aged between 13 and 19 years. To compare how different age groups would become millionaires, we are going to use 10 years from 11-20 years for "Teenager" group in this book.

If investing $500 each year from age 11 to 20, with a total $5,000 invested, the end balance is $773,097, which is less than a million dollars. To get to a million dollars, about $650 each year (or $6,500 total) needs to be invested. The $650 per year can come from your family and/or from the money the teenager made.

While from $6,500 (invested from age 11 to 20 until age 67) to a million dollars is still fantastic, it is not as good as from $5,000 (invested from age 1 to 10 until age 67) to more than 2 million dollars. **This clearly demonstrates the benefit of starting to invest early! A difference in 10 years in these two examples would lead to either a millionaire or a multi-millionaire!**

Table 18: "Teenager" future millionaires (Note: $5,000 invested, $500 each year from age 11 to 20, then held until the age of 67

Age	**$ invested**	**Years invested**	**End balance**	Total balance
11	$500	57	$114,381	$773,097 To get to a million dollars, about $650 each year (or $6500 total) needs to be invested)
12	$500	56	$103,983	
13	$500	55	$94,529	
14	$500	54	$85,935	
15	$500	53	$78,123	
16	$500	52	$71,021	
17	$500	51	$64,564	
18	$500	50	$58,695	
19	$500	49	$53,359	
20	$500	48	$48,508	

Certainly, you don't have to stop at age 20 and can continue to invest more starting from age 21 and to become a multi-millionaire. Next, we will look at examples of starting to invest at the age of 18.

To recap, to possibly reach a million dollars, about $650 each year from age 11 to 20 (or $6500 total) needs to be invested for 48 to 57 years if with an APR of 10%. To possibly reach a multi-million dollars, it is necessary to invest more than $650 per year from age 11 to 20 and/or continue to invest after age 20.

Again, please note this means holding an investment for an extremely long time (48 to 57 years or more) and no tax implications have been considered here. The exact years of becoming a millionaire or a multi-millionaire may also vary due to market volatility and other risks as discussed in Bonus 1 to 5.

Step 3d: Age 18 to start to invest

In the USA, most people finish high school at the age of 18. If you are working full-time starting from the age of 18 or working part-time while going to college, it would be a great idea to start to invest. I did not start to invest until I was 33 (more on this later). I wish I knew to start to invest when I graduated from my high school.

You may ask, how much money should one start to invest from the age of 18? There is certainly not a "one size fit all" answer. We are going to use a few numbers to illustrate the outcome when investing $1,000, or $6,000 or even $12,000 a year.

$1,000 per year is chosen for ease of calculation and hopefully also as an amount that is affordable for most 18 years old.

$6,000 is the annual limit (up to year 2022) that one can contribute to an individual retirement account (IRA). For 2023, the annual IRA contribution limited is $6500.

When you invest in your employer sponsored retirement (such as 401k, 403b, etc.), there is "free money" or "match" from your employer for a portion of the money that you are investing into your retirement plan. The percentage of matches varies from employer to employer, but 6% of matches are common. For someone who makes $50,000 a year, 6% match equals to $3,000 a year. Oftentimes you will have to contribute 6% to get the 6% match. 6% of your contribution and 6% match added up to $6,000 (if your annual salary is $5,0000). This is another reason that $6,000 per year is a good amount to use.

$12,000 is the sum of the $6,000 for IRA (contribution limit in year 2022) & the $6,000 for your employer sponsored retirement plan.

If any of the numbers is not appropriate for your situation, you could simply plug into your desired dollar per year to estimate your investment outcome.

If you start to invest $1,000 per year at age 18 and all the way until the age of 67, the end balance at age 67 will be $1,280,252 (see Table 19). A millionaire is made!

If you start to invest $6,000 per year at age 18 and all the way until the age of 67, the end balance at age 67 will be $7,681,512, or more than 7 million dollars! A multi-millionaire is made!

Obviously, if you start to invest $12,000 per year at age 18 and all the way until the age of 67, the end balance at age 67 will be $15,363,024, or more than 15 million dollars! A multi-millionaire is made!

The other incredible aspect that is worth to pint out is that, if starting at the age of 18 and simply invest $6,000 and another $6,000 at age 19 and stop putting more money into it but hold the $12,000 investment until the age of 67, you will have about 1.3 million dollars ($704,340+$640,308, as shown in table 19)!

Similarly, if investing just one time of $12,000 at the age of 18 and holding it until the age of 67, your $12,000 will grow into about 1.4 million dollars ($704,340*2=$1,408,680, Table 19)! Easy, isn't it?

The examples above are holding the investment until the age of 67. You may also ask how to become a millionaire before the age of 67? From the example above, we know that investing $1,000 per year cannot really make it, what about investing $6,000 or $12,000 a year and how soon can it get to 1 million dollars?

Based on the estimation (by using Excel or from any online investment calculator (e.g., https://www.calculator.net/investment-calculator.html) of investing $6,000 per year and with APR=10%, it will take about 30 years to get to about 1.08 million dollars. This means if starting from the age of 18 and investing $6,000 per year, by the age of 48, you will be a millionaire! Not bad, right?

Similarly, if investing $12,000 per year and with APR=10%, it will take about 23 years to get to about 1.05 million dollars. This means if starting from the age of 18 and investing $12,000 per year, by the age of 41, you will be a millionaire! Fantastic, isn't it?

Table 19. Estimation of $1,000 per year invested, from age 18 and until age 67, APR=10%. With a total of $50,000 invested to become a millionaire with an end balance of $1,280,252. If $6000 invested per year, then it will be $300,000 invested to become a multi-millionaire with an end balance of $7,681,512.

Age	Years invested	End balance	Age	Years invested	End balance
18	50	$117,390	43	25	$10,834
19	49	$106,718	44	24	$9,848
20	48	$97,016	45	23	$8,954
21	47	$88,196	46	22	$8,140
22	46	$80,178	47	21	$7,400
23	45	$72,890	48	20	$6,726
24	44	$66,264	49	19	$6,114
25	43	$60,240	50	18	$5,558
26	42	$54,762	51	17	$5,054
27	41	$49,784	52	16	$4,594
28	40	$45,258	53	15	$4,176
29	39	$41,144	54	14	$3,796
30	38	$37,404	55	13	$3,452
31	37	$34,002	56	12	$3,138
32	36	$30,912	57	11	$2,852
33	35	$28,102	58	10	$2,592
34	34	$25,546	59	9	$2,356
35	33	$23,224	60	8	$2,142
36	32	$21,112	61	7	$1,948
37	31	$19,194	62	6	$1,770
38	30	$17,448	63	5	$1,610
39	29	$15,862	64	4	$1,464
40	28	$14,420	65	3	$1,330
41	27	$13,110	66	2	$1,210
42	26	$11,918	67	1	$1,100
Subtotal		**$1,172094**			**$108,158**
Grand total			**$1,280,252**		

To recap, to start to invest from the age of 18 offers many possibilities of reaching a million dollars or multi-million dollars. One possibility is to simply invest $1000 per year each year until the age of 67 and the end balance may reach about 1.2 million dollars if APR=10%. Another possibility is to invest $6000 each year until the age of 48 and the end balance may reach over million dollars if APR=10%. If continue to invest $6000 per year until the age 67, the end balance will be $7,681,512, clearly a multi-millionaire!

Again, please note this means holding an investment for an extremely long time (30 to 50 years or more) and no tax implications have been considered here. The exact years of becoming a millionaire or a multi-millionaire may also vary due to market volatility and other risks as discussed in Bonus 1 to 5.

Step 3e: Age group 21-30 future millionaires

If investing $500 each year from age 21 to 30, with a total $5,000 invested, the end balance is $298,060, which is less than a million dollars. If investing $1,000 each year from age 21 to 30, with a total $10,000 invested, the end balance is $597,212, which is also less than a million dollars. To get to a million dollars, about $1,678/year from 21 to 30 (or $16,780 total) is needed, if assuming no additional money to be invested after age 30.

Certainly, you don't have to stop at age 30 and can continue to invest more from age 31 and to become a multi-millionaire. Next examples are for starting to invest at the age of 22, an age for most college graduates.

Table 20: Age group 21-30 future millionaires (at the age of 67)

<table>
<tr><th>Age</th><th>$ invested</th><th>Years invested</th><th>End balance</th><th>Total balance</th></tr>
<tr><td>21</td><td>$1,000</td><td>47</td><td>$88,196</td><td rowspan="5">$597,212 (If $10,000 invested, $1,000 each year from age 21 to 30)</td></tr>
<tr><td>22</td><td>$1,000</td><td>46</td><td>$80,178</td></tr>
<tr><td>23</td><td>$1,000</td><td>45</td><td>$72,890</td></tr>
<tr><td>24</td><td>$1,000</td><td>44</td><td>$66,264</td></tr>
<tr><td>25</td><td>$1,000</td><td>43</td><td>$60,240</td></tr>
<tr><td>26</td><td>$1,000</td><td>42</td><td>$54,762</td><td rowspan="5">To get to a million dollars, about $1,678 each year for 10 years (or $16,780 total) needs to be invested</td></tr>
<tr><td>27</td><td>$1,000</td><td>41</td><td>$49,784</td></tr>
<tr><td>28</td><td>$1,000</td><td>40</td><td>$45,258</td></tr>
<tr><td>29</td><td>$1,000</td><td>39</td><td>$41,144</td></tr>
<tr><td>30</td><td>$100</td><td>38</td><td>$37,404</td></tr>
</table>

To recap, if only investing from the age of 21-30 and then hold the investment until the age of 67, to get to a million dollars, ~$1,678 each year for 10 years (or $16,780 total) needs to be invested if APR=10%. Again, please note this means holding an investment for an extremely long time and no tax implications have been considered here. The exact years of becoming a millionaire or a multi-millionaire may also vary due to market volatility and other risks as discussed in Bonus 1 to 5.

Step 3f: Age 22 to start to invest

Another big milestone, now you just turned 22, graduated from college and landed a great job! Congratulations! You may ask how soon can I become a millionaire?

If you start to invest $1,000 per year at age 22 and all the way until 67, the end balance at age 67 will be ~$870k. Not quite a millionaire!

If you start to invest $6,000 per year at age 22 and all the way until 67, the end balance at age 67 will be $5225k. A multi-millionaire is made!

Obviously, if you start to invest $12,000 per year at age 22 and all the way until the age of 67, the end balance at age 67 will be more than 10 million dollars! A multi-millionaire is made!

The other incredible aspect that is worth to pint out is that, if starting at the age of 22 and simply invest $6,000 per year for three years (total $18,000 invested) and stop putting more money into it but hold the $18,000 investment until the age of 67, you could have about 1.2 million dollars!

Similarly, if investing just two times of $12,000 each at the age of 22, 23 and 24, and hold it until the age of 67, your $36,000 will grow into about 2.4 million dollars. Quite remarkable, isn't it?

The examples above are holding the investment until the age of 67. You may also ask how to become a millionaire before the age of 67? From the example above, we know that investing $1,000 per year cannot really make it, what about investing $6,000 or $12,000 a year and how soon can it get to 1 million dollars?

Based on the estimation of investing $6,000 per year and with APR=10%, it will take about 30 years to get to about 1.08 million dollars. This means if starting from the age of 22 and investing $6,000 per year, by the age of 52, you will be a millionaire! Not bad, right?

Similarly, if investing $12,000 per year and with APR=10%, it will take about 23 years to get to about 1.05 million dollars. This means if starting from the age of 22 and invest $12,000 per year, by the age of 45, you will be a millionaire! Fantastic, isn't it?

To recap, to start to invest from the age of 22 offers many possibilities of reaching a million dollars or multi-million dollars. One possibility is to simply invest $6,000 per year for three years (total $18,000 invested) and stop putting more money into it but hold the $18,000 investment until the age of 67, you could have about 1.2 million dollars if APR=10%! Another possibility is to invest $6000 each year until the age of 52 (total $186,000 invested) and the end balance may reach over million dollars if APR=10%.

Similar to age 18 to start to invest. if start to invest at age 22 until the age 67 and with $1000 per year, then the data in Tabel 19 can be used to estimate the total amount of $ invested and the end balance, simply by setting the end balance to $0 for the 1st 4 years (from age 18 to age 21). This will mean that a total of $46,000 invested from the age of 22 to age 67and with an end balance of $870,932 at the age of 67, which is shy of a millionaire. However, if investing $6000 a year from age 22 to age 67, it will be $276,000 invested with an end balance of $5,225,592, also clearly a multi-millionaire!

Again, please note this means holding an investment for an extremely long time (30 years or more) and no tax implications have been considered here. The exact years of becoming a millionaire or a multi-millionaire may also vary due to market volatility and other risks as detailed in Bonus 1 to 5.

Step 3g: Age group 31-40 future millionaires

If investing $500 each year from age 31 to 40, with a total $5,000 invested, the end balance is $114,911, which is less than a million dollars. If investing $1,000 each year from age 31 to 40, with a total of $10,000 invested, the end balance is $229,822, which is also less than a million dollars. To get to a million dollars, about $4,351 each year from age 31 to 40 (or $43,510 total) needs to be invested, if assuming no additional money to be invested after age 40.

Certainly, you don't have to stop at age 40 and can continue to invest more starting from age 31 and to become a multi-millionaire. This is my situation. I did not start to invest until I was 33, I am now still on track to become a multi-millionaire.

Table 21: Age group 31-40 future millionaires (at the age of 67)

<table>
<tr><th>Age</th><th>$ invested</th><th>Years invested</th><th>End balance</th><th>Total balance</th></tr>
<tr><td>31</td><td>$500</td><td>37</td><td>$17,001</td><td rowspan="10">$114,911
(If $5,000 invested, $500 each year from age 31 to 40)

Note: To get to a million dollars, ~$4351 each year for 10 years (or $43510 total) needs to be invested.</td></tr>
<tr><td>32</td><td>$500</td><td>36</td><td>$15,456</td></tr>
<tr><td>33</td><td>$500</td><td>35</td><td>$14,051</td></tr>
<tr><td>34</td><td>$500</td><td>34</td><td>$12,773</td></tr>
<tr><td>35</td><td>$500</td><td>33</td><td>$11,612</td></tr>
<tr><td>36</td><td>$500</td><td>32</td><td>$10,556</td></tr>
<tr><td>37</td><td>$500</td><td>31</td><td>$9,597</td></tr>
<tr><td>38</td><td>$500</td><td>30</td><td>$8,724</td></tr>
<tr><td>39</td><td>$500</td><td>29</td><td>$7,931</td></tr>
<tr><td>40</td><td>$500</td><td>28</td><td>$7,210</td></tr>
</table>

If you start to invest $1,000 per year at age 31 and all the way until 67, the end balance at age 67 will be $363,008. Clearly not a millionaire! If you start to invest $6,000 per year at age 31 and all the way until 67, the end balance at age 67 will be $2,178,048. Still a multi-millionaire!

Obviously, if you start to invest $12,000 per year at age 31 and all the way until the age of 67, the end balance at age 67 will be $4,356,096 or more than 4 million dollars! A multi-millionaire is made!

The examples above are holding the investment until the age of 67. You may also ask how to become a millionaire before the age of 67? From the example above, we know that investing $1,000 per year cannot really make it, what about investing $6,000 or $12,000 a year and how soon can it get to 1 million dollars?

Based on the estimation of investing $6,000 per year and with APR=10%, it will take about 30 years to get to about 1.08 million dollars. This means if starting from the age of 31 and investing $6,000 per year, by the age of 61, you will be a millionaire! Still not too shabby!

Similarly, if investing $12,000 per year and with APR=10%, it will take about 23 years to get to about 1.05 million dollars. This means if starting from the age of 31 and investing $12,000 per year, by the age of 54, you will be a millionaire! Still fabulous, isn't it!

To recap, hopefully you have already started to invest before the age of 31. However, if not, it is still not too late, although it will take more money to be invested each year to reach a millionaire dollar or more.

One possibility is to invest $6,000 per year for 31 years (from age 31 to age 61) (total $186,000 invested), you could have about 1 million dollars at age 61 if APR=10%! If you can invest more, another possibility is to invest $12000 each year until age 54 (total $288,000 invested) and the end balance may reach over million dollars if APR=10%. Continuing to hod the investment from age 54 could enable you to move towards a multi-millionaire.

Again, please note this means holding an investment for an extremely long time and no tax implications have been considered here. The exact years of becoming a millionaire or a multi-millionaire may also vary due to market volatility and other risks as discussed in Bonus 1 to 5.

Step 3h: Age group 41-50 future millionaires

If investing $500 each year from age 41 to 50, with a total $5,000 invested, the end balance is $44,301, which is much less than a million dollars. If investing $1,000 each year from age 41 to 50, with a total of $10,000 invested, the end balance is $88,802, which is also much less than a million dollars. To get to a million dollars, about $11,286 each year from age 41 to 50 (or $112,860 total) needs to be invested, if assuming no additional money to be invested after age 50.

Certainly, most people would have started to invest for retirement before age 41, and you don't have to stop at age 50 and can continue to invest more starting from age 51 and still can become a multi-millionaire.

If you start to invest $1,000 per year at age 41 and all the way until 67, the end balance at age 67 will be only $133,186. Clearly not a millionaire! If you start to invest $6,000 per year at age 41 and all the way until 67, the end balance at age 67 will be $799,116. Still a not a millionaire! However, if you start to invest $12,000 per year at age 41 and all the way until the age of 67, the end balance at age 67 could be about $1.59 million. Still a millionaire is made!

The examples above are holding the investment until the age of 67. You may also ask how to become a millionaire before the age of 67? From the example above, we know that investing $1,000 per year cannot really make it, what about investing $6,000 or $12,000 a year and how soon can it get to 1 million dollars?

Based on the estimation of investing $6,000 per year and with APR=10%, it will take about 30 years to get to about 1.08 million dollars. This means if starting from the age of 41 and investing $6,000 per year, by the age of 71, you will be a millionaire!

Similarly, if investing $12,000 per year and with APR=10%, it will take about 23 years to get to about 1 million dollars. This means if starting from the age of 41 and investing $12,000 per year, by the age of 64, you will be a millionaire! Still not too shabby, isn't it!

Table 22: Age group 41-50 future millionaires (at the age of 67)

Age	$ invested	Years invested	End balance	Total balance
41	$500	27	$6,555	$44,301 (If $5,000 invested, $500 each year from age 41 to 50) To get to a million dollars, about $12000 each year for 10 years ($120000 total) needs to be invested from age 41 to 50 and then hold it until age 67
42	$500	26	$5,959	
43	$500	25	$5,417	
44	$500	24	$4,924	
45	$500	23	$4,477	
46	$500	22	$4,070	
47	$500	21	$3,700	
48	$500	20	$3,363	
49	$500	19	$3,057	
50	$500	18	$2,779	

To recap, hopefully you have already started to invest before the age of 41. However, if not, it is still not too late, although it will take more money to be invested each year to reach a millionaire dollar or more.

One possibility is to invest $12000 each year until age 64 (total $288,000 invested) and the end balance may reach over million dollars if APR=10%.

Again, please note this means holding an investment for an extremely long time and no tax implications have been considered here. The exact years of becoming a millionaire or a multi-millionaire may also vary due to market volatility as discussed in Bonus 1 to 5.

Investing for 23 years is still a very long time, but much shorter than 50 or even 67 years when compared to starting to invest at much younger ages, therefore the potential risk of market volatility is higher.

Step 3i: Age group 51-60 future millionaires

If investing $500 each year from age 51 to 60, with a total $5,000 invested, the end balance is $17,076, which is much less than a million dollars. If investing $1,000 each year from age 51 to 60, with a total $10,000 invested, the end balance is $34,152, which is also much less than a million dollars. To get to a million dollars by age 67, about $29,280 each year from age 51 to 60 (or $292,800 total) needs to be invested, if assuming no additional money to be invested after age 60

If you start to invest $1,000 per year at age 51 and all the way until 67, the end balance at age 67 will be only $44,584. If you start to invest $6,000 per year at age 51 and all the way until 67, the end balance at age 67 will be $267,504. Far from a millionaire! However, if you start to invest $12,000 per year at age 51 and all the way until the age of 67, the end balance at age 67 will be $535,008. Still not a millionaire! This clearly shows the importance of early starting in investment.

Table 23: Age group 51-60 future millionaires (at the age of 67)

Age	**$ invested**	**Years invested**	**End balance**	Total balance
51	$500	17	$2,527	$17,076 (if $5,000 invested, $500 each year from age 51 to 60) To get to a million dollars, ~$29280 each year for 10 years (or $292800 total) needs to be invested and hold it until age 67
52	$500	16	$2,297	
53	$500	15	$2,088	
54	$500	14	$1,898	
55	$500	13	$1,726	
56	$500	12	$1,569	
57	$500	11	$1,426	
58	$500	10	$1,296	
59	$500	9	$1,178	
60	$500	8	$1,071	

Certainly, most people would have started to invest for retirement well before age 51. If for some reason starting from age 51 though, the good news is that you can still make it: if investing $23,000 per year until the age of 67, your investment of $391,000 will grow to about 1.02 million dollars at the age of 67. Or investing $30000 per year for 10 years from age 51 to 60 (a total of $300000 invested) and then hold it until age 67.

To recap, hopefully you have already started to invest before the age of 51. However, if not, it is still possible although it will take much more money to be invested each year to reach a millionaire dollar or more, and the uncertainty of reaching a millionaire dollar or more is much higher due to potential negative impact from market volatility.

Again, please note this means holding an investment for an extremely long time and no tax implications have been considered here. The exact years of becoming a millionaire or a multi-millionaire may also vary due to market volatility as discussed in Bonus 1 to 5.

Investing for 17 years is still a relatively long time, but much shorter than 50 or even 67 years when compared to starting to invest at much younger ages, therefore the potential risk such as market volatility is much higher.

All these examples above were used to illustrate how little or how much more money needs to be invested for how many years to possibly become a millionaire or a multi-millionaire. It is crystal clear that it is possible that everyone can become a millionaire (by the age of 67 or much earlier, depending on when you start to invest and how much money is invested each year). It is also clear that only a small amount of money is needed if starting early.

Please note that all these examples are based on consistently positive APR of 10% over the years and no tax implications have been considered here. This is certainly not necessarily the case and may impact your investment outcome. Please check out the bonus sections for additional details.

SUMMARY

It is often said that "The biggest risk is not taking any risk." or "The biggest risk is inaction."

Everyone could become a millionaire or even a multi-millionaire, simply by following this age-based and easy-to-follow 3-step method as discussed in this book. It is now up to you to evaluate your unique situation, including expectations and realities, such as your investment goals, risk tolerance, age (or time horizon for investing), money available for investing, investing for yourself and/or for your loved ones, etc., and then to decide your appropriate course of investing actions.

Step 1	**Mentality**	To set your mind to believing that you can do it!
Step 2	**Methodology**	To understand the methodology: "magic of the compounding" from the Rule of 72
Step 3	**Actionality**	To start your journey now to harvest the "magic power of the compounding" to become a millionaire or a multi-millionaire, based on your age-group and your unique situation

If you are reading this far, you have already understood the methodology. It is really a matter about how you would like to conduct the step 3, for example, to decide following aspects:

(1) Money: How much money each month or each quarter or each year is available for investing?
(2) Time horizon: What's your age group and how many years would you invest the money?
(3) Do you have the stamina to hold the investment for a very long time (many decades)? Even though the investment may go through many volatile periods.
(4) Which fund or funds to buy? There are numerous investment choices, but there is really no need to get too complicated, simply buying and holding a S&P 500 index fund or ETF would likely be

sufficient, or maybe also investing some money in a NASDAQ ETF (such as QQQ). For more on S&P 500 index and NASDAQ index, please read "Bonus 1" and "Bonus 2".

There are many free online calculators that can be used to help you to estimate mathematically how much money to be invested for how many years to become a millionaire or a multi-millionaire. one of my favorite free online calculators is calculator.net:
https://www.calculator.net/investment-calculator.html
(note: thank the owners of the calculator for giving me permission to use it here).

This calculator allows you to modify the values of flowing parameters:

a. Money: how much money is invested initially (Starting amount) and/or if it is one-time investment (Additional contribution=$0) or recurring investment (Additional contribution=$$)
b. Time horizon: how many years the money will be invested.
c. Return rate: APR, e.g., 10%
d. Contribution and compounding frequency, e.g., monthly, or annually, etc.

Let's use this calculator to do a few estimations.

Estimation #1: one time investment of $1000 or $2000

As seen from the screenshot #1 and #2 (next page) a one-time investment of $1000, if APR=10%, can grow to about $539K after 66 years (see screenshot #1) and to one million dollars after 72.5 years (see screenshot #2). This was the hypothetical scenario for a baby future millionaire as discussed in Step 3a. Obviously, mathematically a one-time investment of $2000 can potentially grow to over one million dollars ($1078k) after 66 years, an example of delayed but much bigger gratification from a hypothetical instant gratification of a $2000 Disney vacation, as discussed in Step 2c (Table 14), $2,000 vacation or a million-dollar vacation?

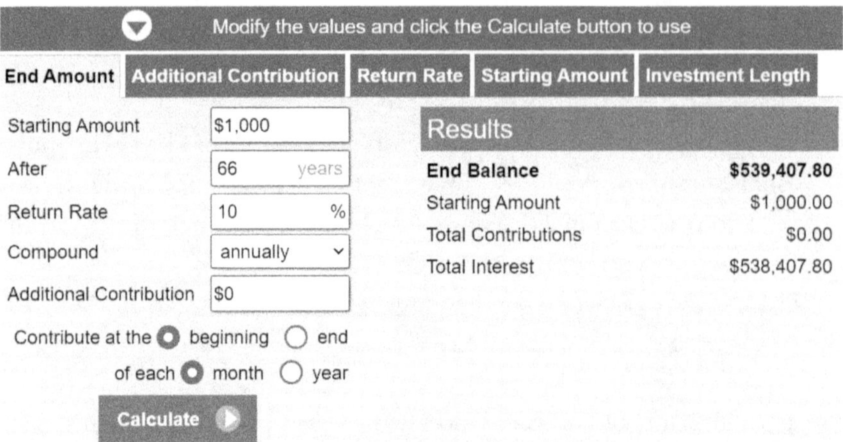

Screenshot #1 (Note: this is in color and easier to read when using this calculator online)

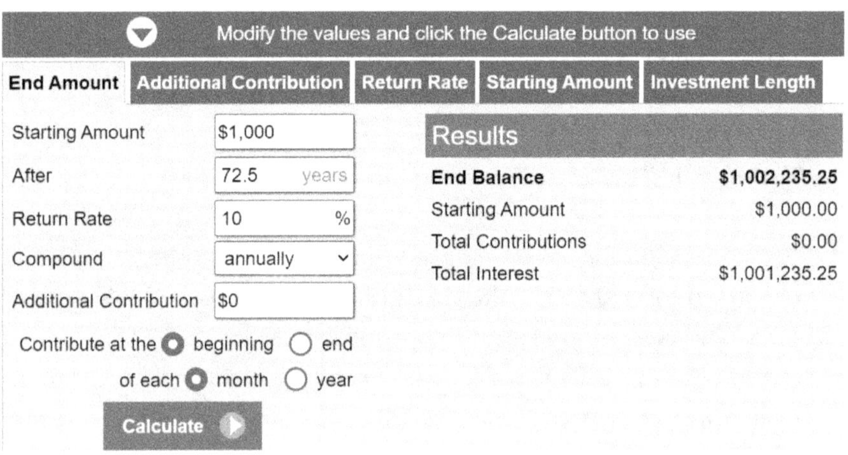

Screenshot #2

Estimation #2: Investments of $500 each year for 4 years

As discussed in Step 3b for the case of young child future millionaire, one scenario is to invest $500 each year for 4 years and hold the investment until age 67. This means the 1st $500 can be invested for 67 years and can grow to ~$296k (if APR=10%, see screenshot #3). The 2nd, 3rd, and 4th $500 can be invested for 66, 65 and 64 years, and will grow to and will grow to ~$269k, ~$245k and ~$222k respectively (screenshots not included). Adding these 4 investments of $500 per year for 4 years together, a total of $2000 investment can potentially grow to a total of over one million dollars after 67 years.

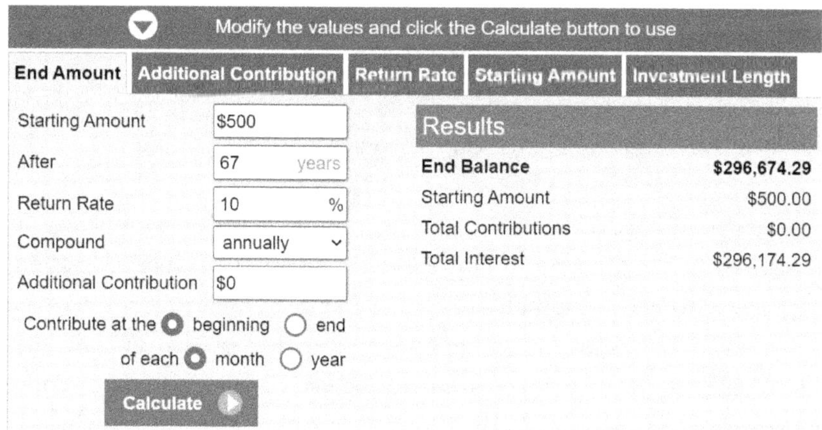

Screenshot #3

Estimation #3: re-occurring investment of $6000 per year.

As discussed in Step 3f, if someone were to start to invest at age 22 and can invest $6000 per year all the way util after age 67, the total amount of money invest over this long period of 46 years (age 22 to age 67) will be $276k and it can mathematically grow to over 5 million dollars (~$5225k, see screenshot #4).

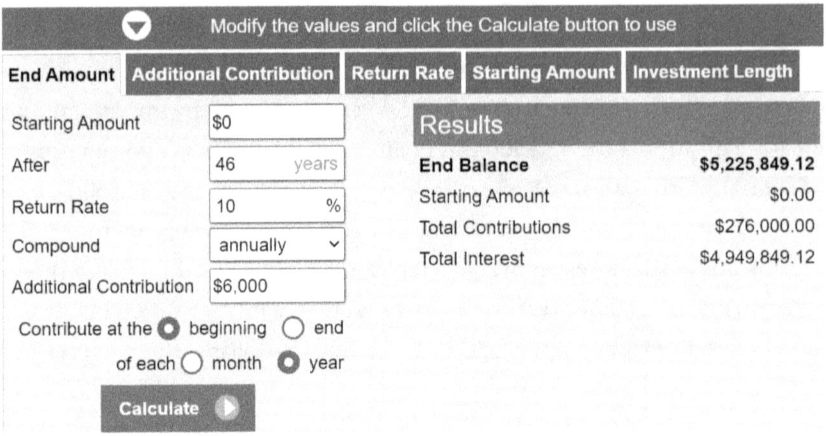

Modify the values and click the Calculate button to use

End Amount | Additional Contribution | Return Rate | Starting Amount | Investment Length

Input	Value
Starting Amount	$0
After	46 years
Return Rate	10 %
Compound	annually
Additional Contribution	$6,000

Contribute at the (•) beginning ( ) end of each ( ) month (•) year

Calculate

Results

End Balance	**$5,225,849.12**
Starting Amount	$0.00
Total Contributions	$276,000.00
Total Interest	$4,949,849.12

Screenshot #4

Above are just a few examples of estimation using the calculator. You can run your own estimation based on your unique situation.

Once you have decided these aspects (money available for investing, time horizon, which investment to buy, etc.), it is just simply a journey of "rinse and repeat" to become a millionaire or even a multi-millionaire. This "rinse and repeat" of investing into either one or more than one investment, either buying once a month or once a quarter or even once a year, is essentially "Dollar-Cost-Average (DCA)" investing over many years until it reaches your investment goal. For more details on DCA, please read "Bonus 3."

It is a long journey, the market would certainly be up and down along the way, there are certainly risks involved and may even lose money over a certain period. Therefore, patience and perseverance over many years or decades are important. Please read "Bonus 4" for a word about investment risks.

For tax advantage, please consider becoming a Roth IRA millionaire or even a Roth IRA multi-millionaire (please read "Bonus 5")!

Wish you a happy and successful journey to your financial independence!

Bonus 1: Reality (historical return of S&P 500) excelled simulation.

In Step 2 and 3, how to become a millionaire or a multi-millionaire is purely based on the estimation or simulation using the Rule of 72 with a consistent APR of 10% over many years. As discussed in Step 2c, the APR of S&P 500 index fluctuates over years. The APR can be negative or positive. Naturally, one would ask how dependable is the simulation in Step 2c? Can one become a millionaire or a multi-millionaire by simply buying and holding an investment such as the S&P 500 index fund?

To answer this question, let's compare the simulation results with the historical return if the same amount of money were to be invested into the S&P 500 index.

The end balance is calculated from simulation with APR=10% and from 4 scenarios: if $1, or $1,000, or $6,000 or $12,000 is invested annually at the beginning of each year for different periods of time, including 10, 20, 30, 40, 50, 60, 67and 95 years.

The end balance (as of the end of year 2022) is also complied from 4 scenarios: if $1, or $1,000, or $6,000 or $12,000 is invested annually into S&P 500 index at the beginning of each year for different periods of time, including 10, 20, 30, 40, 50, 60, 67 and 95 years.

As seen in Table 24, the end balance from simulation is certainly not the same as compared to the end balance if the money were to be invested in S&P 500, it can be higher or lower. The good news is that, except for one period of 30 years, the end balance if invested in S&P 500 is slightly higher (10 or 20 year) or much higher (40, 50, 60, 67, 95 years)!

There may be multiple reasons that that the end balance if invested in S&P 500 is higher than the end balance from the simulation including but not limited to:

(1) The average APR for S&P 500 is 11.7% for the last 95 years (1928-2022), which is higher than 10% used in the simulation.
(2) The fact that more than 70% of the years the APR for S&P 500 is above 0% could be a reason that helps to smooth out the average APR or return over time.
(3) Dollar-Cost-Average (DCA) method of investing helps to smooth out the return over time. More details on DCA in section "Bonus 3".

This means even though the APR of S&P 500 fluctuates over the years, the investment return is outstanding and there are many scenarios where a millionaire or a multi-millionaire is made by simply investing into S&P 500, as detailed below:

(1) For the 10-year period, it is too short a time to get to a millionaire, when the annual investment is capped at $12,000.
(2) For the 20-year period, with $12,000 invested annually, the end balance is $760,728, which is not too far from a million dollars. If $15,800 were invested annually for the 20-year period, it does get to one million dollars.
(3) For the 30-year period, even though the outcome is worse than simulated using 10% APY, the end balance is still close to a million dollars to over a million dollars: $905,115 with $6,000 invested annually in S&P 500, and an end balance of $1,810,231 with $12,000 invested annually. Still well-done!
(4) For the 40-year period, a multi-millionaire is easily made: over 3 million dollars with $6,000 invested annually, and over 6 million dollars with $12,000 invested annually. Excellent!

    This is very encouraging when considering following two aspects:

    a. This is most applicable to the ones who start to work at the age of 22 and will have 44 years to invest until the age of 67.
    b. It is an extremely easy way to invest, simply buying the S&P 500 index each year. In this example, it is bought just once a year, either $6,000 or $12,000. But it may be more practical to spread the investment monthly (either $500 per month or $1,000 per month) using the Dollar-Cost-Average (DCA) method.

Interestingly, either investing via DCA once a year or via DCA once a month into the S&P 500 index has almost identical return. More on DCA in section "Bonus 3".

Table 24. Simulation (SPY 10%) vs. Investment return of S&P 500 index over the last 10 to 95 years. Note this is calculated based on the average annual return of the S&P 500 index and re-occurring investment of equal amount at the beginning of each year. The $ is rounded up to the nearest thousand (k) dollar.

$ invested /Year	Years invested	S&P Average APR	$ Invested total	End balance from simulation APY 10%	End balance (2022) if invested in S&P 500	Difference (SPY - simulation)
$1	10	13.7% (2013-2022)	$10	$17.50	$18.20	$0.70
$1k			$10k	$17.5k	$18.20	$700
$6k			$60k	$105k	$109k	$4k
$12k			$120k	$210k	$218k	$8k
$1	20	11.3% (2003-2022)	$20	$63	$63.40	$0.40
$1k			$20k	$63k	$63.4k	$400
$6k			$120k	$378k	$380k	$2.4k
$12k			$240k	$756k	$760k	$4k
$1	30	11.3% (1993-2022)	$30	$180	$150	($30)
$1k			$30k	$180k	$150k	-$30k
$6k			$180k	$1,085k	$905k	-$180k
$12k			$360k	$2,171k	$1,810k	-$361k
$1	40	12.7% (1983-2022)	$40	$486	$530	$44
$1k			$40k	$486k	$530k	$44k
$6k			$240k	$2,921k	$3,184k	$263k
$12k			$480k	$5,842k	$6,368k	$526k
$1	50	11.9% (1973-2022)	$50	$1,280	$1,861	$581
$1k			$50k	$1,280k	$1,861k	$581k
$6k			$300k	$7,681k	$11,170k	$3,488k
$12k			$600k	$15,363k	$22,339k	$6,976k
$1	60	11.7% (1963-2022)	$60	$3,338	$4,096	$758
$1k			$60k	$3,338k	$4,096k	$758k
$6k			$360k	$20,029k	$24,576k	$4,547k
$12k			$720k	$40,059k	$49,153k	$9,094k
$1	67	11.5% (1956-2022)	$67	$6,516	$7,521	$1,005
$1k			$67k	$6,515k	$7,521k	$1,005k
$6k			$402k	$39,095k	$45,128k	$6,033k
$12k			$804k	$78,190k	$90,256k	$12,066k
$1	95	11.7% (1928-2022)	$93	$94k	$159k	$65k
$1k			$93k	$94k	$159,363k	$65,250k
$6k			$558k	$94,112k	$956,178k	$391,503k
$12k			$1,116k	$564,674k	$1,912,356k	$783,007k

(5) Similarly for the 50-year period, multi-millionaire is easily made: over 2 million dollars with just $1,000 invested annually, over 11 million dollars with $6,000 invested annually, and over 22 million dollars with $12,000 invested annually. Fantastic!
This scenario is wonderful since is most applicable to the ones who start to work at the age of 18 and will have almost 50 years to invest until the age of 67. And the money invested annually can also be lower, e.g., just $1,000 annually.

(6) For the 60-year period, obviously a multi-millionaire is easily made. Although 60 years is such a long time and not all of us may need start to cash out some of our investment before 60 years, it is still very meaningful for at least two situations:
   a. If you started to invest in your baby, the investment can certainly be held for 60 years or longer.
   b. for the people started to invest at the age of 18 or 22, 60 years mean it is now age 78 or 82, a portion of the investment could still be invested for 60 years or even longer.

(7) For the 67-year and 95-year period, if you are lucky to be able to hold the investment for that long, you are then very wealthy, and the focus is now different and is on your legacy on how much wealth you could leave it to your children and society.

In summary, while the simulation may seem too good to be true, the real data from the S&P 500 index benchmark, even with widely fluctuated APR and a recent terrible year of 2022, affirms that it is true that everyone can become a millionaire or a multi-millionaire, by simply following the age-based and easy-to-follow 3-step approach as detailed in this book.

Note: while it is possible that everyone can become a millionaire or a multi-millionaire, by simply following the age-based and easy-to-follow 3-step approach as detailed in this book, the time periods (or the number of years) to achieve that may not necessarily be identical to what was discussed in Table 24, since the past return is not indictive of future performance and therefore future APR may be different.

Bonus 2: Other possible investment choices in addition to S&P 500

There are numerous investment choices in the stock market, including mutual funds, ETFs, individual stocks, or bonds., etc. In the United States, there are thousands of funds (e.g., more than 7,000 mutual funds and more than 7,000 ETFs) and thousands on stocks. In addition to the stock market, there are also other investment choices such as real estate investment, gold, etc. You may think it is too hard and/or too risky to invest. Or you may think only professionals in the financial industry can do it. One can certainly make the investment choices as complicated as you would like, but there is really no need to. Step 3 showed you how to keep the investment choice extremely simple by buying and holding the S& P 500 index only, so everyone can do it.

The S&P 500 index fund as a benchmark has with overall average APR (from 1928 to 2022) of 11.7%. As discussed in "Bonus 1" section, simply buying, and holding a S&P 500 index will enable you to become a millionaire or a multi-millionaire.

However, one may ask if it is possible to get a higher APR than simply investing in S&P 500? While there is no clear answer to this question, many people and investment companies have devoted a lot of effort into this with mixed results. Peter Lynch, the author of "One up on Wall Street," is one of the most successful and well-known investors. He ran the Fidelity Magellan fund from 1977 to 1990. Peter managed to beat the market (or the S&P 50 index) 11 out of 13 years by a huge margin and was able to achieve an average APR of >29%! However, most of the funds underperformed the S&P 500. For example, usually more than 60% of the actively managed stock funds underperformed the S&P 500. It gets worse with longer time: after 10 years, 85% of the large cap funds underperformed the S&P 500, and after 15 years, almost 92% of the funds are trailing the S&P 500 index.

Clearly, it is very hard to outperform S&P 500. One may need to take on more risks (e.g., by investing in individual stocks and/or by investing in aggressive growth funds) for potentially higher reruns. Note that taking on more risk is not a guarantee to achieve higher return and may lead to lower return due to loss of money from some risky investment choices.

However, if you are still not content with the return offered by S&P 500, the following research is supplied for your info for consideration, even though it is not considered as a guarantee to achieve higher return than just investing in S&P 500.

As shown in table 25 (see next page), for the last 10 years or 20 years, investment in QQQ did better than in SPY.

There is some overlapping in holdings between S&P 500 index and NASDAQ index (or QQQ). In addition, QQQ has limited track record in terms of years, I can only find data starting from 1999 (rom Yahoo Finance website), as compared to a long track record of S&P 500 (data available starting from 1928)

Even though investing in QQQ did better than in SPY in the last 10 to 20 years, it does not guarantee from now on that investing in QQQ will do better than in S&P 500. And it is worth noting that during the crash of sot.com in early 2000, QQQ has three consecutive years of negative returns: -36.93% in 2000, -32.78% in 2001 and -37.66% in 2002. These negative returns clearly showed that investment in the tech heavy index can be risky, even though the technology sector may have potential to grow faster. In this regard, if you have high risk tolerance, it may be worth considering investing some of the money into QQQ, an exchange-traded fund that tracks the NASDAQ 100 Index or even QQQJ, an exchange-traded fund that tracks the next generation NASDAQ 100 index. Please note that QQQJ invests in smaller tech companies as compared to QQQ and therefore may be riskier than investing in QQQ. Please also note that QQQJ is a brand-new ETF that started in October 2020 and therefore there is very limited data available.

Please note the QQQ data discussed here only serves as an example of possible additional investment choice in addition to S&P 500. The author is not affiliated with QQQ or QQQJ. As already mentioned, there are numerous investment choices and each investment choice may have a different risk profile, please do your homework to choose your additional investment choices if you are not content to just simply invest in S&P 500.

Table 25. Investment return of S&P 500 index vs. NASDAQ (QQQ) over the last 10 years (2013-2022) or 20 years (2003-2022). If assuming $1, $1,000, $6,000 or $12,000 invested each year starting from 2003 and then held until the end of 2022.

$ invested /year	**Years Invested**	**Average APR**	**$ Invested total**	**End balance if invested in S&P**	**End balance if invested in QQQ**	**Difference**
$1	10	13.7% (SPY) 18.7% (QQQ)	$10	$18	$22	$4
$1k			$10k	$18k	$21k	$3k
$6k			$60k	$109k	$130k	$21k
$12k			$120k	$218k	$261k	$42k
$1	20	11.4% (SPY) 16.4% (QQQ)	$20	$63	$99	$35
$1k			$20k	$63k	$98k	$35k
$6k			$120k	$380k	$591k	$211k
$12k			$240k	$760k	$1,182k	$422k

Please stay tuned to my next book on how investments other than SPY or QQQ could help to build a multi-million-dollar portfolio. While the book title has not been finalized yet, it could be something like "10 stocks to build a multi-million-dollar portfolio." The plan is to start a real money portfolio in early 2024, by selecting 10 stocks and using DCA (see Bonus 3) method to invest a certain amount of money on a monthly basis. If investing $1000 monthly, the projection (based on historical return) is that it will reach 2 million dollars or more in 30 years. The portfolio will be reviewed every 5 and 10 years against market return to see how the portfolio is doing against the projected goal.

Bonus 3: Dollar-Cost-Average (DCA)

Dollar-Cost-Average (DCA) is an investing method in which an investor does not invest the total amount of money all at one time but divides the total amount of money up to be invested many times across months or even years. This method is an effort to reduce the impact of volatility. It may lead to lower the average cost for overall purchase in a down market but may not necessarily be beneficial in an up market. Let us illustrate this from the following examples:

Example #1: This example compares two scenarios for NASDAQ invested in 2000 and held until the end of 2020.

(1) One time investment (no DCA): Hypothetically, if you have only $1 to invest and invested in NASDAQ on March 10th, 2,000, this $1 would grow 155% to $2.55 by the end of 2020.

(2) DCA (Dollar-cost-average over two investments): However, if you invested $0.5 in NASDAQ on March 10th, 2,000, and $0.5 in NASDAQ on Oct. 9th, 2002, the 1st $0.5 each would grow 155%, and the 2nd $0.5 each would grow 1056%, in total the $1 would grow to $7.05.

In this example, $1 across the two purchases using DCA method grows to $7.05, much better than the one-time purchase (not using DCA) that grew to $2.55.

In example #1, the second purchase was at exactly the **lowest point** of NASDAQ (or lowest cost base) which is very difficult to do. In example #2, let us use another example to illustrate the potential benefit of DCA that does not require to make purchase at the lowest point of the market.

Example #2: This example compares two scenarios for NASDAQ invested in 2001 and held until the end of 2020.

(1) One time investment (no DCA): $1200 invested one time in NASDAQ at the beginning of 2001 and held until the end of 2020. The $1200 has a gain of 365.3% and grew to $5583.
(2) DCA monthly (Dollar-cost-average over 12 months): $1200 invested in NASDAQ during 2001, with $100 each month and held until the end of 2020. The $1200 has an average gain of 557.6% and grew to $7892.

In this example, the DCA from the 12 purchases has shown clear benefit (with an ending balance of $7892 with DCA vs. $5583 without using DCA) since the NASDAQ price dropped considerably from the beginning of 2001 to the end of 2001.

Table 26: DCA example #2. The end balance is calculated based on a monthly investment of $100 for 12 months ($1200 total) and held until the end of 2020. The end balance from DCA is $7892, vs. $5583 from a one-time investment (no DCA) of $1200 at the beginning of the year.

Date	Adj Close	Adj Close 30-Dec-2020	% Gain/Loss	End balance
1/1/2001	$2,773	12,900.28	365.3%	$465
2/1/2001	$2,152		499.5%	$600
3/1/2001	$1,840		601.1%	$701
4/1/2001	$2,116		509.7%	$610
5/1/2001	$2,110		511.4%	$611
6/1/2001	$2,161		497.3%	$597
7/1/2001	$2,027		536.7%	$637
8/1/2001	$1,805		614.9%	$715
9/1/2001	$1,499		761.2%	$861
10/1/2001	$1,690		663.8%	$764
11/1/2001	$1,931		568.7%	$669
12/1/2001	$1,950		562.0%	$662
Average			**557.6%**	
Total				**$7,892**

Example #3: This example compares two scenarios for NASDAQ invested in 2005 and held until the end of 2020.

(1) One time investment (no DCA): $1200 invested one time in NASDAQ at the beginning of 2005 and held until the end of 2020. The $1200 has a gain of 527.8% and grew to $7534.
(2) DCA monthly (Dollar-cost-average over 12 months): $1200 invested in NASDAQ during 2005, with $100 each month and held until the end of 2020. The $1200 has an average gain of 487.6% and grew to $7413.

In this example, the DCA over the 12 purchases is not as good as just one purchase, although the difference is not big (minus $121, $7413 vs $7534).

Table 27: DCA example #3. The end balance is calculated based on a monthly investment of $100 for 12 months ($1200 total invested). The end balance from DCA is $7413, as compared to $7534 from a one-time investment (no DCA) of $1200 at the beginning of the year.

Date	Adj close	Adj Close 30-Dec-2020	% Gain/Loss	End balance
1/1/2005	$2,062	12,948.28	**527.8%**	$628
2/1/2005	$2,052		531.1%	$631
3/1/2005	$1,999		547.8%	$648
4/1/2005	$1,922		574.0%	$674
5/1/2005	$2,068		526.3%	$626
6/1/2005	$2,057		529.7%	$630
7/1/2005	$2,185		492.9%	$593
8/1/2005	$2,152		502.0%	$602
9/1/2005	$2,152		502.1%	$602
10/1/2005	$2,120		511.1%	$611
11/1/2005	$2,233		480.4%	$580
12/1/2005	$2,205		487.6%	$588
Average			**517.70%**	
Total				**$7,413**

Example #4. This example compares two scenarios for S&P500 invested in 2020 and held until the end of 2020.

(1) One time investment (no DCA): $1200 invested one time in S&P 500 at the beginning of 2020 and held until the end of 2020. The $1200 has a gain of 14.6% and grew to $1375.
(2) DCA monthly (Dollar-cost-average over 12 months): $1200 invested in S&P500 during 2020, with $100 each month and held until the end of 2020. The $1200 has an average gain of 18.3% and grew to $1419.

In this example, the DCA over the 12 purchases as showed some benefit.

Table 28: DCA example #4. The end balance is calculated based on a monthly investment of $100 for 12 months ($1200 total invested). The end balance from DCA is $1419.1, as compared to $1375 from a one-time investment (no DCA) of $1200 at the beginning of the year.

Date	Adj close	Adj Close 30-Dec-2020	% Gain/Loss	End balance
1/1/2020	$3,258		**14.6%**	$114.6
2/1/2020	$3,249		14.9%	$114.9
3/1/2020	$3,090		20.8%	$120.8
4/1/2020	$2,471		51.1%	$151.1
5/1/2020	$2,831		31.8%	$131.8
6/1/2020	$3,056		22.1%	$122.1
7/1/2020	$3,116		19.8%	$119.8
8/1/2020	$3,295	3,732.04	13.3%	$113.3
9/1/2020	$3,527		5.8%	$105.8
10/1/2020	$3,381		10.4%	$110.4
11/1/2020	$3,310		12.7%	$112.7
12/1/2020	$3,662		1.9%	$101.9
Average	**$1,200**		**18.3%**	
Total				**$1,419.1**

These examples have shown the potential benefits and potential downsides of the dollar cost average (DCA) method. **In real life, since the money available for investing is usually earned overtime, using DCA method is practical.**

Bonus 4: A word about investment risks

Investing in a stock market is not FDIC insured and may lose money. There are many risks associated with investing:

(1) Market risk: an investment may decrease in value due to undesirable economic news or other events such as interest rate changes, geopolitical tension including wars, natural disasters, public health crisis, etc. For example, During the dot-com bubble, the Nasdaq index rose ~400% from 1995 to March 2,000 then to fall ~78% from the peak in 2,000 to 2002. During the 2020 pandemic, the S&P 500 index lost about 34% from February 19th, 2020, to March 20th, 2020. And most recently in 2022, S&P 500 index lost close to 20%, and NASDAQ index lost more than 30%.

The market risk may impact on your overall investment return. As discussed in Bonus 1, the average APR for S&P 500 is 11.7% for the last 95 years (1928-2022), which is higher than the 10% used in the simulation. However, past return is not an indication of future return. If the APR is only 6%, not the 10% used in many of the examples, the overall return will be lower.

As an example, while $2000 invested for 66years in APR of 10% can grow to over one million dollars, if the APR is only 6%, $2000 invested for 66 years can only grow to $93587 (see screenshot #5), which is much less than one million dollars.

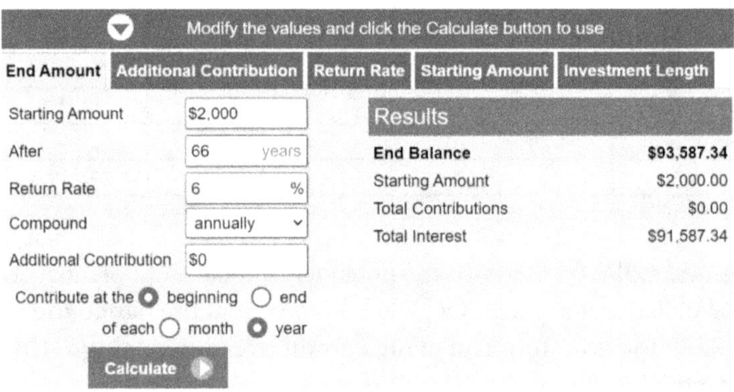

Screenshot #5

(2) Inflation risk: Overtime, the cost of goods and services increase. This is inflation that means a dollar can buy fewer goods or less services as time goes on. There is a risk of losing purchasing power if investment return does not keep up with inflation rate. 2022 is a year with high inflation.

(3) Asset allocation risk: there is a risk if all the money is concentrated on one investment or one type of investment. This is like putting all the eggs in one basket. If the basket falls, all eggs may break. One example of this is the recent failure of Silicon Valley bank stock (SVB), with a brief timeline below:

March 8th (Wednesday) 2023: Silicon Valley Bank announced a loss of $1.8 billion.

March 9th (Thursday) 2023: SVB stock crashed: SVB lost more than 60% in a single day, from about $268 a share to about $106 a share. As the panic spreads through social media, people start to pull their money out of Silicon Valley Bank.

March 10th (Friday) 2023: after a premarket selloff, the trading of SVB shares were halted Friday morning. Soon after, federal regulators announced they have taken control of the bank. It is the second-biggest bank failure in U.S. history, after Washington Mutual's collapse during the height of the 2008 financial crisis.

(4) Political and geographic risks: Changing of political environment and wars may negatively impact the return of investments.

(5) Personal health risk: worrying about the risk of losing money from investing may increase stress and affect one's health. Worrying about not investing (and therefore may not have enough money for different needs) may do the same.

How to then minimize investment risks?

(1) Adequate time horizon
Investment can be risky and volatile in a short period of time. The longer the time horizon, the lower the risk.

Not all the money should be invested in the stock market. The portion of the money that is needed for the next 3-5 years should not be invested in the stock market. Take the same example of the dot-com bubble, if someone were to start to invest into NASDAQ index from the peak of bubble around early 2,000, by 2002, the NASDAQ index lost about 78% of its value. If you need the money and were to sell in 2002, then a huge loss would occur. However, if you don't need the money and keep it invested, the 78% loss is on a loss on the paper for that period from 2002 to 2002, it is not a real loss. Even though it took until the end of 2014 for the NASDAQ index to battle back to its March 2,000 level, if keep it invested until the end of 2020, a nice gain or a huge gain is realized (Table 29): 155% since March 2002 and 1056% since October 2002.

Table 29: NASDAQ gain and loss since the dot-com bubble

Date	NASDAQ close	Period	Years	Gain/ loss %
3/10/2000	5048.62			
10/9/2002	1114.11	March 2000 to Oct 2002	<3	-78%
4/23/2015	5056.06	March 2000 to April 2015	~15	~0%
		Oct. 2002 to Dec. 2015	~13	354%
12/30/2022	10466.48	March 2000 to Dec 2022	~22	107%
		Oct. 2002 to Dec. 2022	~20	839%

The NASDAQ historical data clearly proved that, although not guaranteed, most of the times, the longer the time horizon, potentially the lower the risk and the higher return. To harvest the magic power of compounding, investment should be held for a long period of time.

(2) Dollar cost average (DCA)
Investing overtime using the dollar-cost-average (DCA) method discussed in "Bonus 3" could help to reduce the risk.

(3) Diversification

Diversification is an investing method to lower risk by "putting eggs in multiple baskets." By diversifying investments across a range of different companies, industries, sector or asset classes, your investment is not concentrated in a single company, industry, sector, or asset class. Different companies, industries and asset classes have different risk profiles, therefore overall risk is lowered.

During the dot-com bubble, NASDAQ dropped about 78%. During the same period, S&P dropped about 43%, which is still a huge drop, but not as bad as NASDAQ. In the year 2020, S&P gained 14.6%, but NASDAQ gained 43.6%. Clearly, if one were only to invest in NASDAQ and S&P500, pending on asset allocation (or % allocated) between these two indexes, the investment outcome would be different.

Additionally, diversification may also include investing some of your money outside the stock markets, such as in bonds, real estate, art, collectibles, etc. Especially when someone is approaching retirement age, it is usually recommended not to have 100% of your investment portfolio in stocks, but allocated between stocks and bonds, such as 60% stocks/40% bonds or 50% stocks/50% bonds or 40% stocks/60% bonds, etc., based on your age and risk tolerance.

(4) Possibility to minimize personal health risk from investing: the sleep factor.
To minimize the stress associated with investment risks, one should be examining your unique situation and risk tolerance level carefully. If an investing decision (for example, either taking on too much risk or worry about inflation risk because not investing at all) is impacting your sleep, re-evaluate your situation and decision so you can sleep soundly at night by only taking on calculated risks.

Bonus 5: A word about tax: the wonderful Roth IRA millionaires!

It is often said that there are wo things in the world that cannot be avoided, one is death, the other one is tax. The good news is that some tax can be minimized in the USA, per the current law and if the law does not change in the future.

In the USA, the gain from investing may be taxable. For the example of baby millionaires discussed in step 3, $2,000 invested after many years may grow to $1,078,814. The gain in this example is $1,076,814 which is taxable.

How can one become a millionaire or multi-millionaire and keep all the money (not having to pay tax)? The answer is in Roth IRA

Currently in the USA (using year 2022 as an example), one can invest up to $6,000 per year into an individual retirement account (IRA), the $6,000 must come from earned income. There are two types of IRAs. One of them is a traditional IRA in which the $6,000 contribution may be tax deductible depending on your income, but the gain from the traditional IRA is taxable. The other one is Roth IRA in which the $6,000 contribution is not tax deductible, and the gain is also not taxable. This means that, if you follow the IRA contribution and withdrawal Rules (which can be found online), the whole ROTH IRA account balance is not taxable, and you got to keep all the money!

Following investing scenarios (already discussed in Step 3), but being invested into a Roth IRA account, could make you a Roth IRA millionaire or a multi-millionaire.

If you start to invest $6,000 per year at age 22 into a Roth IRA account and all the way until 67, the end balance at age 67 will be over ~$5.18 million. A multi-millionaire is made!

The other incredible aspect is that, if starting at the age of 22 and simply invest $6k per year for three years (total $18k invested) and stop putting more money into it but hold the $18k investment in a Roth IRA account until the age of 67, you will have about 1.3 million dollars.

The examples above are holding the investment until the age of 67. You may also ask how to become a Roth IRA millionaire before the age of 67? Based on the estimation of investing $6,000 per year and with APR=10%, it will take about 30 years to get to about 1.19 million dollars. This means if starting from the age of 22 and investing $6,000 per year, by the age of 52, you will be already a Roth IRA millionaire!

In addition to Traditional IRA/Roth IRA, there are other investments that have tax advantage (tax-deferred, and/or free of taxes). Some of them are listed below. The details are out of scope for this book, please research online if interested in knowing more details.

Health Savings Account (HSA)
529 Education Fund.
401(k)/403(b) Employer-Sponsored Retirement Plan.
Municipal Bonds.
Tax-free Exchange Traded Funds (ETF)
U.S. Series I Savings Bond.
Charitable Donations

Appendix #1: Compounding growth of $1 over 80 years (if APR10%)

After years	Value ($)	Total gain ($)	Total return %
1	$1.10	$0.10	10%
2	$1.21	$0.21	21%
3	$1.33	$0.33	33%
4	$1.46	$0.46	46%
5	$1.61	$0.61	61%
6	$1.77	$0.77	77%
7	$1.95	$0.95	95%
8	$2.14	$1.14	114%
9	$2.36	$1.36	136%
10	$2.59	$1.59	159%
11	$2.85	$1.85	185%
12	$3.14	$2.14	214%
13	$3.45	$2.45	245%
14	$3.80	$2.80	280%
15	$4.18	$3.18	318%
16	$4.59	$3.59	359%
17	$5.05	$4.05	405%
18	$5.56	$4.56	456%
19	$6.12	$5.12	512%
20	$6.73	$5.73	573%
21	$7.40	$6.40	640%
22	$8.14	$7.14	714%
23	$8.95	$7.95	795%
24	$9.85	$8.85	885%
25	$10.83	$9.83	983%
26	$11.92	$10.92	1092%
27	$13.11	$12.11	1211%
28	$14.42	$13.42	1342%
29	$15.86	$14.86	1486%
30	$17.45	$16.45	1645%
31	$19.19	$18.19	1819%
32	$21.11	$20.11	2011%
33	$23.23	$22.23	2223%
34	$25.55	$24.55	2455%
35	$28.10	$27.10	2710%
36	$30.91	$29.91	2991%
37	$34.00	$33.00	3300%
38	$37.40	$36.40	3640%

39	$41.14	$40.14	4014%
40	$45.26	$44.26	4426%
41	$49.79	$48.79	4879%
42	$54.76	$53.76	5376%
43	$60.24	$59.24	5924%
44	$66.26	$65.26	6526%
45	$72.89	$71.89	7189%
46	$80.18	$79.18	7918%
47	$88.20	$87.20	8720%
48	$97.02	$96.02	9602%
49	$106.72	$105.72	10572%
50	$117.39	$116.39	11639%
51	$129.13	$128.13	12813%
52	$142.04	$141.04	14104%
53	$156.25	$155.25	15525%
54	$171.87	$170.87	17087%
55	$189.06	$188.06	18806%
56	$207.97	$206.97	20697%
57	$228.76	$227.76	22776%
58	$251.64	$250.64	25064%
59	$276.80	$275.80	27580%
60	$304.48	$303.48	30348%
61	$334.93	$333.93	33393%
62	$368.42	$367.42	36742%
63	$405.27	$404.27	40427%
64	$445.79	$444.79	44479%
65	$490.37	$489.37	48937%
66	$539.41	$538.41	53841%
67	$593.35	$592.35	59235%
68	$652.68	$651.68	65168%
69	$717.95	$716.95	71695%
70	$789.75	$788.75	78875%
71	$868.72	$867.72	86772%
72	$955.59	$954.59	95459%
73	$1,051.15	$1,050.15	105015%
74	$1,156.27	$1,155.27	115527%
75	$1,271.90	$1,270.90	127090%
76	$1,399.08	$1,398.08	139808%
77	$1,538.99	$1,537.99	153799%
78	$1,692.89	$1,691.89	169189%
79	$1,862.18	$1,861.18	186118%
80	$2,048.40	$2,047.40	204740%

Index

About the author

After my Ph.D. degree, the author taught for about two years at a university, then did two post-doctoral research projects, one in Germany and one in the USA, before starting to work for a biomedical device/pharmaceutical company.

Working an industry job and with paychecks as the only income, there was always a sense of insecurity financially. Therefore, the author devoted countless hours to self-learn personal investing and discovered an incredibly easy method of building wealth OVER MANY YEARS by taking advantage of the "magic" of compounding growth based on the "Rule of 72". Since then, this knowledge and this simple and easy-to-follow three-step method as detailed in this book has helped the author achieve finical independence and therefore also a sense of security financially.

As mentioned in the introduction of this book, it is sad that only a small percentage of the people are millionaires here in the USA, because virtually everyone can become a millionaire based on the author's own experience and the easy-to-follow three-step method as detailed in this book, regardless of your education level and/or background (the author is a scientist and not someone who works on Wall Street), once made aware of the "rule of 72" and have the patience to follow through, can then easily use this knowledge and this aged based three-step method to help to build wealth over a long period of time.

That is why it is exciting to share this knowledge, and this simply-to-follow, age-based three-step method with you, to help you also harvest the "magic" of compounding growth based on the "Rule of 72", and to help more people like you to become millionaires or to become better-off financially.

Thanks for reading and best wishes!

Please stay tuned for my next book: "10 stocks to build a multi-million-dollar portfolio." Note that the book title may change and see more details in "Bonus 2."

www.ingramcontent.com/pod-product-compliance
Lightning Source LLC
LaVergne TN
LVHW010940110826
845149LV00013B/2692
* 9 7 9 8 9 8 9 6 5 4 1 0 9 *